HISTORY as HIGH ADVENTURE

HISTORY

as high

ADVENTURE

by

WALTER PRESCOTT WEBB

Edited with an introduction by
E. C. BARKSDALE

AUSTIN • 1969

Publication of the Jenkins Garrett Foundation by
THE PEMBERTON PRESS

INTRODUCTION to the SERIES

FOR SOME time it has been our hope and dream to publish historically significant documents and other material in the Foundation's library that have never been published or whose publication is not readily available outside the larger libraries.

This volume represents the first tangible step toward the realization of this dream. It is appropriate that this initial publication contains speeches of Walter Prescott Webb. It was out of a love for and an appreciation of the relevance and high adventure of history, kindled in a history class of Dr. Webb's at the University of Texas, that the Foundation's library had its beginning.

We are most grateful for the encouragement, enthusiasm and support of Mrs. Walter P. Webb, Dr. Harry Ransom, and Dr. E. C. Barksdale in making this work a reality.

It was found that the vicissitudes of publications are legion. Our esteem for The Pemberton Press and men of like valor has been greatly heightened in the past year.

Jenkins Garrett Foundation

CONTENTS

An EXPLANATION

"AN HONEST PREFACE," Walter Prescott Webb's minor masterpiece, should have put an end to all prefaces. Unfortunately, it did not.[1] In an attempt to beat Satan around an ox-yoke or call a dirty damned shovel a computerized excavating utensil, this prologue is, therefore, not "Preface" but "An Explanation."

The present volume is, I understand, the first in a series which will make available to those interested some of the gleanings in the outstanding private collection of the Jenkins Garrett Foundation. In the selections no claim is made to literary excellence, to unearthed secrets, nor to startling disclosure. The merit, if any, rests in the fact that there is presented relatively rare material which, with some exceptions, is not available to the general reader in hard-backed form. In brief, some of the speeches contained herein have appeared in print elsewhere, notably Webb's two inaugural addresses before learned societies. The reason for their inclusion will be noted later. Generally, however, the "pieces" are found in typewritten or mimeographed form only, or have appeared in publications of limited circulation, mostly are out of print. One in particular, "Learning and Wisdom: the Relevance of History," is, or so I have been informed, the only copy extant.

Much has been written about Webb. Some of it is good, some bad, some indifferent. Much remains to be written. Because of his impact on the thought of the Western World, much needs to be written. I predict, for example, that his *Great Frontier* should and eventually will take its rightful place on the book shelves which display Western man's greatest wisdom, a work to be ranked with *The Wealth of Nations*, *The Evolution of Species*, *Principia*, or *Das Kapital*.

Those in charge of graduate historical seminars suffer, perhaps, from an overdose of modesty. They write about others, not themselves. They send their students out to search for facts about some obscure historical actor of no great pith or moment and ignore the more worthy members of their own at times colorful and often significant breed. Webb, though essentially a modest man, was not guilty of this fault. He wrote about the original development of his ideas and about how he wrote. Evidence appears repeatedly in this collection of essays. His *Harper's Magazine* article, "The Search for William E. Hind,"[2] was autobiographical. He had intimated to close friends shortly before his untimely death that he was thinking of an autobiography. If this is so, tragedy on the old San Antonio-Austin highway denied to us that value. In short, the definitive biography of Webb remains unwritten. It should be written. I have a worthy candidate for the job, but thus far he has not accepted the nomination.

Despite his asseveration that he was lazy, and in spite of some published comments that his contributions were scant, Webb wrote a great deal. His bibliography in *Texas Libraries*[3] occupies more than five pages. That in The Brick Row

Book Shop catalogue[4] fills almost nine pages. The most recent and comprehensive compilation, by Francine Morris of The University of Texas: Arlington Library, to be published in the University of Texas Press edition of the first "Webb Memorial Lectures,"[5] includes some fourteen pages of typescript. Much of what he wrote was significant. Some of it was pedestrian, "made" work, for example, a few of his brief newspaper articles on a trip he made through the West. All, however, had his distinctive touch. His main theses, as all Webb students know, rested on good Earth foundations, on geoeconomic themes: local in the *Texas Rangers*; regional in *Divided We Stand*, and in his various speeches and articles on the South, the West, and the desert; continental in the *Great Plains*; and international in the *Great Frontier*. He was, however, many-faceted. In his maturity he was an urbane cosmopolite and yet always with some of the demeanor and curiosity—and appearance—of a country farm boy.

Webb's driving obsession is shown in his great ideas. Yet he found plenty of time to be interested in and occasionally to write about many things: the work of a relic-hunter on the Gulf Coast, an East Texas school teacher with pupils in the third grade, a beetle which had the curious ability successfully to prognosticate the outcome of horse races as reported in the *Saturday Evening Post*, the disc plow of a Texan-Norwegian whom he called a Swede, sea gulls in Salt Lake City, a school for "stick men" or croupiers who supervised dice shooters in Las Vegas, log cabins, grass, dry wells, six-shooters, windmills, Yorkshire pigs, boys' camps, fine wines, Old Forester, great works of literature, feuds, and indigent university students. He could advise and did advise many college presidents, some governors, and one who was to become President of the United States. Yet at the same time, he could listen to and often heed the counsel of Afro-American yard men, random stock brokers, itinerant book salesmen, draggle-tailed college sophomores, and one fortune teller. I have sworn off in this "Explanation" anecdotes concerning him. They are myriad and will grow and be embellished and fancified with the passing years. One, however, points indirectly to his catholic interests and essential modesty. Breckenridge, Texas, was a hotbed of high school football success at a time when Webb's own university was in the athletic doldrums. While he stopped for lunch in a leading Breckenridge cafe during a slack period, the waitress, prompted by a question from Webb's companion, gave the interested professor a play by play account of the past three Breckenridge games together with the names, weights, habits, and a glowing description of abilities of all the players. Finally, she thought of her "manners" and politely asked Dr. Webb,

"Where you frum?"

"The University of Texas at Austin."

Reprovingly, she commented, "You ain't had much of a football team down there for some time."

"Maybe," said Dr. Webb grinning, "we believe in education 'down there'."

"Hrumph," she snorted, staring at him. "You must!" Then she added reflectively, "I hope you ain't a fair sample."

Webb shook the table with his laughter. "You know," he said later on the road, "that waitress ought to be a book reviewer for some of the learned journals."

Webb was proud of being a historian. To him the profession should not be that of an academician, the fabled egghead. He introduced with pride the phrase, "As a Professional Historian I . . . ." He stated that his only technical writing ability lay in the field of exposition, that he was not a novelist or a poet, though he had tried his hand at poetasting once when as a very young man he thought he was in love. Webb did not think of himself as possessed of the lyric gift, yet some of his passages sang:

And there it is, clothed in magic, a vision of truth never perceived so clearly by any other man.[6]

Or from "The Art of Historical Writing":

And so, as we linger in contemplation of the great tapestry of modern literature which has left us images of what the human imagination did with a New World, we know that it represents a special kind of experience, that it is done, and our last impression as we turn away is that to many of us it was as big as God.[7]

Belying his bromo-quinine visage, Webb was ordinarily the mildest and kindliest of men, but when a principle was at stake and he was stirred he could be as savage as a John Randolph of Roanoke or Harold Ickes. His resolution on filling the Presidency of The University of Texas, during one of its more troubled episodes, whether right or wrong, and I think it was right, required courage of the highest order and split the faculty down the middle.

But enough about Webb. Let his writings speak for him. Many anthologists have a compulsion to explain reasons for their inclusions and excisions. This "Explanation" follows briefly their hackneyed trail. The theme is found in the address from which the title of the volume is derived: "History As High Adventure." Thus, in this collection the selections, with one exception, bear a relationship, usually though not always direct between Webb and history. Later works in the series may include his thoughts on the South, the North, the West, the Desert, bookmaking, soft drink vending machines, marble toilets and other subjects of greater or less moment, but this one deals with History.

The first essay appeared as an editorial in the *Junior Historian*, a magazine of an organization founded by Webb which J. Frank Dobie said might prove to be Webb's greatest contribution. In the editorial Webb defines the function of History as well as it has even been defined, saying in essence and in his colorful vernacular that History, the pedigree of mankind, should be as important to humanity as is the pedigree of a stud horse to a Palomino breeder.

For the purposes of contrast, next is included the culmination of Webb's formal academic career, his inaugural address as President of the American Historical Association delivered in New York in 1958. It and Webb's other inaugural, "The Historical Seminar: Its Outer Shell and Its Inner Spirit," delivered in 1953 to the Mississippi Valley Historical Association, now known as the Organization of American Historians, are the only selections in this volume which are widely available, appearing in several other sources. They are familiar to all who have studied Webb and thus are not rare, though the thought in them is rare. They are included because they, and especially "History Is High Adventure," are, in the opinion of many, the high-water mark of Webb's shorter contributions. I have heard Historians who have attended the meetings of many professional societies state that "History As High Adventure" is one of the greatest "papers" they have ever heard. Much of "History As High Adventure" is the end result of whetting and honing and strapping and polishing other Webb material, some of which was published earlier and a good bit of which appears in one form or another and sometimes verbatim in other selections herein.

In the next several selections—"The Story of Some Prairie Inventions," "Physics and History," "Geographical-Historical Concepts in American History," and "A Texas Museum of Natural History"—Webb with different introductions and conclusions plays the themes which were consummated for him, if not for subsequent investigators, in *The Great Frontier* and *The Great Plains*—the importance of earth and the importance of tools on earth, or, to coin a fancy phrase of the kind popular among those who like to attach a jaw-breaking name to a simple but fundamental concept: the "geo-physical-utilitarian-environmental-concept-of-history-and-a-place-in-which-to-put-it." I would add that it is the "macro-economic" view of History, except that I do not know what "macro-economic" means. The selection "Geographical-Historical Concepts in American History" was delivered in 1960 to the annual meeting of the Association of American Geographers. Particularly interesting is Webb's proposal that Houston build a great museum of natural history which would show the impact of land, of geography and of natural resources on the culture and architecture—and history—of Texas. Ignorance forces me to confess that I do not know whether the great city on the Ship Channel has adopted and expanded on the Webb suggestion. I do know that it has built an Astrodome. Curiously, an amusement center in Arlington, Texas, "Six Flags Over Texas," sometimes called "The Texas Disneyland," has, in part at least, used some ramifications of the Webb idea, a panorama of Texas presented as a carnival ride, and that as a result "Six Flags" grosses several millions of dollars in admission fees annually.

Come we next to material which in essence embodies Webb's ideas on history writing, history courses, history teaching, history students, and history teachers, leading off with "The Historical Seminar: Its Outer Shell and Its Inner Spirit," his Mississippi Valley inaugural, and concluding with an article delivered before a writer's conference and which weirdly enough has, apparently in Webb's own handwriting, the date June 5, 1964, a year after his death. In these addresses Webb ranges through a wide field of peripheral matter touching upon the historian's profession. He mentions such godheads in the field as Leopold von Ranke of Germany. He delivers delightful and acerbic comments to a session of The American Historical Association on nonindigenous history professors in Texas. Webb did not like the educational fetish still current in Texas against inbreeding, the belief that Texans are not fit to teach history in Texas higher institutions of learning. This attitude of his was based, presumably, on the philosophy inherent in the story of the young hillbilly who allegedly told his father that he could not marry his intended "cawse she's a virgin, Paw," to be met with the parental response, "Yore sho' right, son. If she ain't good enuff'n for her own folk she ain't good enuff for we'uns." He comments on his own University's non-Texan faculty Committee's refusal to allow him $84.70 for travel expenses to an American Historical Association meeting to read a paper on "University Historians and History Teachers." The refusal was predicated, he thought, on the failure of non-Texan university professors to be much interested in undergraduate teaching or in the subject of history in Texas secondary and elementary schools or to catalogue these non-important matters under the sacred heading of "research." He discusses his early reading interest in "Witch Crow and Barney Bylow" and "Jack the Giant Killer," pays his respects to certain forms of academic research, and ends with a tribute to a no-longer-young East Texas schoolmarm who wrote an acceptable thesis for him. He wished repeatedly that she would conclude a book which she had tentatively titled *Thirty Years in the Third Grade*.

The final selections—"Learning and Wisdom: The Relevance of History" and "The Great Frontier: An Interpretation"—might well be in an appendix. Much of their substance, ideas and some of the same illustrations and exact words appear in other contributions. "Learning and Wisdom: the Relevance of History," delivered to a Southern Methodist University Seminar, is, I understand, the only copy. "The Great Frontier: An Interpretation," delivered before an audience in Muncie, Indiana, though not his last is one of Webb's final papers. It contains, something rare for Webb, brief mention of and only reply to some of the criticisms of his monumental *Great Frontier*.

A beautiful book (and the adjective is used advisedly) both in format and content is *Toward the Morning Sun*, published by the Dean of the Graduate School of The University of Texas: Austin. The title is taken from a sentence in the *Great Plains*. The book, a limited edition, contains words by Webb, tributes to Webb, and reproductions of paintings in the Webb spirit by Tom Lea. This is not the place for another eulogy of Webb. Enough have been delivered. I shall conclude simply by saying that if one reads carefully all the selections contained in the present volume he will get a belly full of history. As with a fine meal prepared by a master chef, however, the reader should not suffer indigestion, because Webb at his greatest could and did point man's—and woman's—imagination and philosophy toward the splendor that can be reflected from the light of early day, toward the morning sun.

E. C. Barksdale

I The FUNCTION of HISTORY

THE FUNCTION of history, as I see it, is to describe and make understandable the forces which have shaped the destiny of man and brought him to the present time equipped as he now is with his ideas and institutions. Prehistoric man carried little baggage; present day man staggers under his load of ideas, institutions and tools which have been gathered slowly and painfully in the long march from *then* to *now*. History is the record of how, when and where man acquired this baggage which we call civilization. History is an invoice of a bill of goods acquired by purchase and inheritance from the past and offered to man in the market of the immediate and distant future.

What I have said seems to apply to history, whether global, national, state, or local. All of the worthy aims and high purposes stated for history are latent in the general principles laid down.

If what I have said is true, then it should be quite clear why intelligent men and women are interested in history. They are interested for the same reason that a merchant is interested in the invoice, price and qualities of the goods placed on his shelves. The intelligent ranchman is much concerned with the pedigree of his Hereford bull and his palomino stud. Every breeder is interested in the pedigree—which is simply the history—of what he breeds. Man breeds in addition to his own kind something we call civilization. History is the pedigree of that civilization and culture.

We would think it very strange of any man who would pay a high price for a thoroughbred and not demand the papers with the horse. The papers do not make the thoroughbred a better horse, but they do make him far more valuable to the owner and more interesting to others. History is the "papers" of man; it is the register of his lineage, the record of his performance, and the guarantee of his qualities.

II HISTORY as HIGH ADVENTURE

HIS IS the seventy-second presidential address delivered before the American Historical Association. The previous seventy-one were prepared by seventy persons. Naturally, as the game proceeds, the selection of a subject becomes increasingly difficult, because the first-comers harvested the tallest grain, leaving to us later ones the gleaning of well-mown fields. The presidents have dwelt with the usefulness of history, with the facts, the fallacies, the vagaries, the science, the philosophy, the content, and with the individuals who support the great man theory; they have examined imagination, faith, freedom, distinction, religion, and even truth.

He who scans these contributions feels that there is little left to say on the more serious aspects of history. In fact, he finds in what has already been said a good deal of repetition and a considerable amount of contradiction.

Two rifts I have been able to detect in this cloud of learning, two opportunities not yet pre-empted. The first is in the field of humor. Judging by the published addresses, one must conclude that historians are deadly serious when called upon to give testimony of their stewardship. There is, so far as I have been able to find, scarcely a glimmer of humor, hardly a particle of wit, and rarely a suggestion of exuberant spirit in the whole collection. The historian, reading these addresses seventy-five years hence, will see that presidents had much learning, some wisdom, and no fun at all. Since I am not qualified, either by nature or by inclination, to fill this gap with a little laughter, I leave that joyous task to a bolder successor.

The second opening, the one I shall enter, lies in the field of personal experience, of adventure into that great wilderness of the past, that wild country wherein one can be lost for days or weeks or months, in exploration as exciting as any known to argonauts or *conquistadores*; and the lovely feature about this delirious experience is that the historical explorer moves among the dangers and hardships with complete immunity until finally he comes out in print, in point-blank range of the critics. It does seem strange that the historians have been so unwilling to relate their personal experience in historical exploration. They have tended to hide themselves in anonymity, to be impersonal, to give a blueprint of their fragment of truth rather than the enthralling tale of how it was chased, cornered, and captured. What I tell here makes no claim to objectivity. It is designed to be as subjective and revealing as I can make it, and yet have within as much truth as one can afford when talking about himself.

Here I need to warn those young historians who flock to these meetings, apparently in the hope that they will gain some clue on getting forward in this profession. They are likely to think that the man who is president may reveal the secret of how he got there. Presidents in their turn seem to be influenced by what is expected of them, and so they give something of their philosophy of history which more often than not exhibits how they felt after they got there. While I, as some of my predecessors have done, am talking tonight out of at least one side of my mouth to these young historians, I would tell them, and I want to tell them with emphasis, that if they aspire to occupy this place, they should listen attentively to my story, make notes on my education, graduate record, and college career, and then be extremely careful to avoid following the example of one who has done nearly everything wrong. Seeing what I have done, they will know what not to do.

My presence here is one of the most improbable accidents in the history of the profession. I am here in defiance of geography, regionalism, and history. My background is southern, both parents being from Mississippi; my home is west of the Big River, and my field of study has been the plebeian field of Western America. All my degrees are from a state university, the one in which I teach. I have never taught anywhere else except temporarily. I am one of the few persons who did not have to leave home to get a job. I am an example of institutional inbreeding which frightens all universities save the two that practice it most, Harvard and Oxford.

Of my seventy-two presidential predecessors, seventy were American citizens, one Canadian, and one French. Of the seventy Americans, sixty-three came from the northern states, two from the South, and five from the West. Patrick Henry's grandson, the seventh president, was elected from Virginia in 1891. I am the only person ever elected while a teacher in a southern institution. Two presidents were born west of the Mississippi River, but I am the only one of them elected to the office while a resident teacher west of the river.

Though California has furnished five presidents, all of them were transplanted from the East save the one who was from England. If any young man here is ambitious to be president, he should shun the South and avoid the West. The ambitious designer of a charted career should bear in mind that two states, New York and Massachusetts, have furnished thirty-six presidents, one-half of the total, and that the percentage will increase.

I could tell a great deal about my predecessors, that the average age is sixty-three, that two were in their eighties, thirteen in their seventies, thirty-two in their sixties, and two, Jameson and Turner, in their forties. The office has been held by such distinguished people as presidents and ambassadors and by natives of England, Scotland, France, Canada, Scandinavia, and Russia.

When I pointed out to my wife that 90 percent of the presidents were from the North and suggested that she should be very proud that at last the South had also been recognized, she replied with one of those marvelous flashes of misunderstanding, "I know—they have decided to integrate!"

Since I promised a human story, I will refrain from statistics. It would be highly gratifying if I could say that from a very early age I wanted to be a historian, and that I bent every effort to this purpose. Nothing could be further from the truth. Actually I have never been ambitious in the profession, as witnessed by the fact that I have a poor record of attendance at the national meetings, have served on no committees, written few book reviews, and have never submitted an article to either of the national journals, although a former presidential address was published. This indifference illustrates two points: first, that I never expected national recognition; second, that I have followed my own interests, acquiring in the process severe penalties and an occasional reward.

What I wanted to be was a writer, and I wanted to write, not for the few but for the many, never for the specialist who doesn't read much anyway. I wanted to write so that people could understand me; I wanted to persuade them, lure them along from sentence to paragraph, make them see patterns of truth in the kaleidoscope of the past, exercise upon them the marvelous magic of words as conveyors of thought. With this ambition to write I entered college, very late and with little preparation, and here my past caught up with me. I convinced

6

several English professors that I could not punctuate, and they convinced me that I could not write. For years I did not touch pen to paper.

In my junior year I registered for a course called Institutional History, taught by a Canadian-born and European-trained scholar, Lindley Miller Keasbey. What he taught was not history, nor economics, nor anthropology, nor philosophy, but a good deal of all these and more. He swept me off my feet, gave me a method of thinking and a point of view which has entered into all that I have done. His patterns were clear, concise, and exciting. I took all his courses and decided that I would become a teacher of institutional history, beginning in the high schools. But when I surveyed the field, as a wiser person would have done earlier, I found that there was no such thing as institutional history except in The University of Texas. Then I learned that this man was so unorthodox that he was not welcomed to teach in any standard department. To provide a place for him, the authorities allowed him to set up an independent department and his former colleagues were dismayed when their best students flocked to him by the hundreds. The authorities finally solved the problem and restored harmony by firing him. And there I was, a specialist in a non-existent field of learning.

But on the record institutional history does look like history, enough like it to fool one school board. Thus I became a history teacher with only two elementary courses in the subject. Now, since I was making a living teaching history, I decided it would be wise to learn something about it, and I began taking advanced courses, and finally took the B.A. degree at about the age most take the Ph.D. In the meantime I had made something of a reputation as a high school teacher of history, and had written an article on the subject, and that made me an expert. In 1918 I was invited to The University of Texas to conduct a course in the teaching of history so that it would not be given by a methodologist.

The time had come to start work on the M.A. It was

necessary to choose a subject, and here good fortune attended me. A series of Mexican revolutions had made the Texas border a turbulent place; James E. Ferguson as governor had made all Texas turbulent. Ferguson increased the Ranger force, and the Rangers went to the border to commit crimes almost as numerous and quite as heinous as Pancho Villa bandits. These crimes were exposed in a legislative investigation led by J. T. Canales. The exposure made exciting headlines in all the papers. I read those headlines and asked myself an important question: Has anyone written the history of the Texas Rangers? The answer was no. I chose that subject and was off on the first lap of the great adventure, to write the history of the oldest institution of its kind in the world. The story led west, to the frontier, to vicarious adventure of the body, and to real adventure of the mind. Though I was not aware of it then, I had found my field.

Trailing the Texas Rangers, who in turn had trailed the ancestors of some of the best people in Texas, was a combination of drudgery and fun. It was my first work with sources, the faded letters and reports of a handful of men standing between the people and their enemies, men better with a gun than with a pen. Though the records were abundant, I did not stop with the records. Like Parkman I went to all the places where things had happened. I sought out the old men, still living then, who had fought Comanches and Apaches, killed Sam Bass at Round Rock, and broken up deadly feuds inherited from the more deadly reconstruction. With a captain and a private I visited every Ranger camp on the Mexican border where there were still elements of danger; I carried a commission and had the exhilarating experience of wearing a Colt revolver in places where it might have been useful. At night by the campfires I listened to the tales told by men who could talk without notes.

Though the desire to write had been suppressed, it had not been killed. One day I sat down and wrote an article sketching the early history of the Texas Rangers, and for the

8

first time an editor paid me the compliment of writing a check in my favor. This was a landmark, the beginning of a long and happy relationship between me and editors. In retrospect I wondered what had enabled me to break the barrier separating academic people from paying editors. Why had my early efforts been rejected? What new element had entered which enabled me to persuade an editor to write a check? The difference was that now I had something to say; I had learned intimately about one segment of life. The subject I had found in my own front yard was one that I could understand as I could never understand such exotic, to me, topics as the French Revolution or Renaissance art. The way led west.

It was during these same years that the oil boom broke in West Texas. It began in my home town of Ranger, a village of one thousand which became a brawling mass of ten thousand in six months. Law and order broke down, the criminal element rushed in to gamble, murder, and rob. Then the Rangers came to run out the criminals and restore local government to the demoralized citizens. This was a formula repeated in town after town as the boom spread. The genuine boom was followed by a bogus one, run by speculators who floated stock promotions to fleece the gullible public.

One of these bogus companies with headquarters in Fort Worth founded a magazine and decided to do a series of articles on the services the Texas Rangers had rendered in cleaning up the oil towns. The editor addressed a letter to the University asking who was qualified to write the story. The letter found its way to my desk, and I began to tell the story of my Rangers at two cents a word. This pleasant arrangement was interrupted by a United States marshal and judge who had quaint ideas about the uses of the mail.

Though I did not realize it at the time, as I tell this story Texas does seem to have been an exciting place. I shall always be grateful to this crooked oil company because in writing articles for it I stumbled on one of the few original ideas I ever had. As a matter of fact up until that time I had

9

never had one.

This idea came to me on a dark winter night when a heavy rain was rattling on the roof of the small back room where I was trying to write an article for the oil magazine. By this time I knew a great deal about the Texas Rangers, their dependence on horses and their love for the Colt revolver; I knew the nature of their enemies, primarily the Comanches, and I knew the kind of society they represented and defended. I was ready for that moment of synthesis that comes after long hours of aimless research to give understanding and animation to inert knowledge. What I saw that night was that when Stephen F. Austin brought his colonists to Texas, he brought them to the edge of one environment, the eastern woodland, and to the border of another environment, the Great Plains. The Texas Rangers were called into existence and kept in existence primarily to defend the settlements against Indians on horseback, Indians equipped with weapons that could be used on horseback. These Texans, fresh from the forests, had no such weapons for theirs had been developed in the woods and were not suited for horsemen. While the conflict between the Ranger and the Comanches was at its height, Samuel Colt invented the revolver, the ideal weapon for a man on horseback. It took a year to gather the proof of what I knew that night, and I sensed that something very important happened when the American people emerged from the woodland and undertook to live on the plains. In that transition the Texans were the forerunners, the Rangers the spearhead of the advance, and the revolver an adaptation to the needs of a new situation.

The excitement of that moment was probably the greatest creative sensation I have ever known. With the roar of the rain in my ears, I went to the front of the house to tell the most sympathetic listener I have known that I had come upon something really important, that I was no longer an imitator, parroting what I read or what some professor had said. This idea that something happened when the Americans

10

came out of the woods and undertook to live on the plains freed me from authority, and set me out on an independent course of inquiry. One question I asked over and over, of myself and of others: What else happened? What other changes took place in the manner of living when thousands of westbound people emerged from a humid, broken woodland to live on the level, semi-arid plains where there was never enough water and practically no wood? This question attended me in all my reading, and led straight to the books I needed. In this chase the Texas Rangers, formerly so exciting, became dull and prosaic fellows, and I cast them aside to follow the new trail that still led west. The teaching of Keasbey came back in full force as I studied the western environment and tried to find its effect on human beings.

Though I had picked up the M.A. degree in transit, I still lacked the accursed Ph.D. The pressure to get it was gentle, for that was a tolerant age, but it was there, and I was advised to go elsewhere for graduate work. That is wise advice for most people, but it came near being fatal for me. I was already too old, and what is more, I now had an idea of my own which made others—to my teeming mind at that moment—seem of secondary importance. My adviser, Frederic Duncalf, wrote to Professor Turner about a scholarship at Harvard, but Turner replied saying I was too old and should not try Harvard. I shall always be grateful to Turner for this favor and for reasons that will be apparent later. Chicago was less discriminating, and I was fortunate in going where no one offered a course in western history.

At the end of twelve months I returned to Texas ill, deep in debt, and without the degree. I would have preferred to omit this adventure, but the academic grapevine has carried the story, somewhat distorted, far and wide, and I dare not ignore it completely. There should be a moral here, but the only one I can find is this: don't take an original idea into a graduate school.

The trip back to Texas after a long absence is one I shall

not forget. At St. Louis, I boarded the San Antonio car of the Texas Special where I heard again familiar voices of people I never knew talking in familiar accents of cotton, cattle, and oil. I was already home.

I brought home some stout resolutions: (1) I would never listen to another academic lecture if I could help it; (2) I would recoup my finances; (3) I would henceforth follow my own intellectual interests at whatever cost; (4) I would write history as I saw it from Texas, and not as it appeared in some distant center of learning. Thanks to the tolerance of my department, I did not have to listen to any more academic lectures. I recouped my finances by participating in a series of highly successful textbooks, a wonderful antidote for academic anemia. Then I turned from textbooks and a small fortune to write history as I saw it from Texas. The road led west, and I now knew I had something to say.

A few people have asked why I remained in Texas, as if that were something needing explanation. The obvious answer should be clear from what has been said. The real answer is that I was bound to Texas by many ties. All the sources I needed were there, and those for the Texas Rangers existed nowhere else. Also the key to understanding the American West up to 1875 was there. It was in Texas that the Anglo-Americans first tackled the problem of living on the plains; it was there they made the first adjustments, such as learning how to fight on horseback and how to handle cattle from horses. The processes of this adjustment that I was slowly discovering could be perceived more clearly from the south end of the plains corridor than from any other vantage point. And of course when I returned to Texas without the degree I was not in a favorable position to be considered elsewhere. My situation was like that of Mr. George B. Dealey, who began work as an errand boy in a Texas newspaper office and wound up later as owner of what became a truly great newspaper. "Why, Mr. Dealey," an admirer asked, "did you happen to stay in Texas?" "The answer is very simple," Mr. Dealey said. "No one offered me a job."

Without design, I was now on the way to becoming a western historian. I was excellently prepared because I had never had a course in that field, and therefore could view it without preconceived notions or borrowed points of view. With an instinct for the possible, I had stumbled into the least complex area of the United States where there were no industries as in the North, no special institutions as in the South, no battlefields or statesmen, and only local politics. Practically all the records were in English so that the language requirements were negligible.

Slight as the demands were, I was ill prepared to meet them. My idea of the compelling unity of the American West had now become an obsession. That unity was exemplified in the geology, the geography, the climate, vegetation, animal life and Indian life, all background forces operating with telling effect on those people who in the nineteenth century crawled out of the salubrious eastern woodland to live in this harsh land. To the problem of understanding this Western environment in all its aspects, I applied the technique learned from Keasbey. This technique consisted of taking an environment, in this case the Great Plains, as a unit, and superimposing layer after layer of its components with geology as the foundation and the latest human culture, literature, as the final product, the flower growing out of the compost of human effort and physical forces. There was a compelling logic in this plan for him who would follow it, but to plough through such unknown fields as geology, climatology, botany, anthropology to arrive finally at the sixteenth century—when men began to make a record of their puny efforts, many failures and few successes—in order to write the heroic and tragic history of the American West, was no small task. But it was high adventure. I have never worked so hard or with such exaltation as in those days when I carved out of the books piece after piece of folklore or science or history and found that they all fit together to form a harmonious pattern

13

which I knew beforehand was there.

Yes, this was the easy field. No matter how hard I worked, I was still a western historian. No one understood the trouble or the fun I was having in relating the many fields to my topic. In commenting one day to a colleague in a more scholarly division of history, I said: "Never have I felt so keenly the need of an education. The fact that I didn't get one is most unfortunate!"

"Yes," he said, "but think how lucky you were in getting into a field where you don't need it!"

In two respects I was indeed lucky. (1) In the Great Plains I had chosen an environment simple in structure whose force was so compelling as to influence profoundly whatever touched it. The trail was plain, and the technique learned from Keasbey was applicable. (2) I was also lucky in that I was examining for meaning a familiar land which I had known as a child. A friend asked me once when I began preparation to write *The Great Plains*. I answered that I began at the age of four when my father left the humid East and set his family down in West Texas, on the very edge of the open, arid country which stretched north and west farther than a boy could imagine. There I touched the hem of the garment of the real frontier; there I tasted alkali. I was not the first man, or boy; but the first men, Indian fighters, buffalo hunters, trail-drivers, half-reformed outlaws, and Oklahoma boomers were all around, full of memories and eloquent in relating them to small boys. There I saw the crops burned by drought, eaten by grasshoppers, and destroyed by hail. I felt the seering winds come furnace-hot from the desert to destroy in a day the hopes of a year, and I saw a trail herd blinded and crazy from thirst completely out of control of horse-weary cowboys with faces so drawn they looked like death masks. In the hard-packed yard and on the encircling red-stone hills was the geology, in the pasture the desert botany and all the wild animals of the plains save the buffalo. The Indians, the fierce Comanches, had so recently

14

departed, leaving memories so vivid and tales so harrowing that their red ghosts, lurking in every mott and hollow, drove me home all prickly with fear when I ventured too far. The whole Great Plains was there in microcosm, and the book I wrote was but an extension and explanation of what I had known first hand in miniature, in a sense an autobiography with scholarly trimmings.

The Great Plains was published in 1931, and no more need be said about it except that it has never been revised, never will be revised by me, never has been imitated, and I am told by the publisher it never will go out of print. I came out of the experience of writing it—doing something in my own way—with a sense of power that comes to him who has made a long journey for a purpose, overcome the hardships, and returned to tell with appropriate exaggeration what to him is an important tale.

I was forty-three years old and still without the degree. There was nothing to do but turn back to the Texas Rangers which had been thrown aside in the excitement of exploring the Great Plains. At this stage Dr. Eugene C. Barker suggested that I use *The Great Plains* as a dissertation and take the degree at The University of Texas. I objected because I thought more of the book than that; it was not a dissertation, and I doubt the subject would have been accepted by any discreet department in the country.[1]

It was necessary to go through some mumbo jumbo to satisfy the regulations, but this was done with proper decorum and the degree was given to me a year later. I did not even earn it. I have sat on many doctoral committees, always spiritually very near the cornered candidate, and I have never sat on one where I could have passed the examination. I have, as my colleagues know, I am sure, been a pushover for people who have trouble answering silly questions.

The Texas Rangers was published in 1935, eighteen years after I started it. The writing of a book is an act of resolution. At some stage the author must say: "No more

15

research. I will not be lured away by new material. I will write this damned thing now." What led me to this resolution and held me to the task was the realization that 1935 would mark the hundredth anniversary of the Texas Rangers, and the next year Texas would celebrate with fanfare and much false history the centennial of its independence.

Though it takes resolution to begin a book, it takes more to complete it. There are dark moments when the struggling author wonders why he began it, and if it is worthwhile anyway. There are times when he is lost in the dark forest of alternatives. He can't go forward and he can't go back. Fred Gipson, author of *Hound-Dog Man*, tells a story to illustrate this crisis as he experienced it. After World War I, a neighbor took a contract to drive 3,000 head of goats 150 miles through the hill country of Texas. The only help he could get was Fred, aged sixteen, and another boy aged thirteen. The day after the drive started, the autumn rains set in and continued for three weeks. A goat is a self-willed brute, essentially a desert animal, averse to the dousing effect of water and reluctant to travel in the rain. When 3,000 goats hump up and refuse to move under prodding, it makes a problem for the man and two boys who have to move them.

The rain had soaked the clothes, the bedding, put out the campfires, and mildewed the food; it had made the soles come loose on the boys' shoes so that they had to be tied on with binding twine and baling wire. Tempers wore thin. The smaller boy threw a stick at a humped up goat and broke its leg. The boss, completely exhausted himself, lost his temper, and gave the boy the roughest tongue lashing he had ever had. Fred said he can never forget the picture of abject misery this boy made as he stood, the rain running off his flop hat, his face distorted with anger and hurt, his tears as copious as the rain. When the boss was out of earshot, he made a futile gesture of despair, and said, "Dammit, Fred, if I knew the way home, I'd quit." So would many an author.

But if one persists, both goats and books can be delivered.

Since *The Texas Rangers* was the only book about Texas that appeared in 1935, Paramount bought it for the Texas Centennial picture of 1936. Paramount made full use of the title, and little else. The picture was quite successful. I am not going to tell you what I got for it in the midst of the depression, but I will say this: what I got made the depression more tolerable.

My next adventure, *Divided We Stand*, published in 1937, guaranteed that I would never be called to a Northern university. I knew this when I wrote it, but I was doing pretty well where I was. The book has been called a pamphlet, a philippic, and a good many other things. Because the people could read it and did, it was not objective. It was based on the simple device of dividing the country into three sections, the North, the South, and the West, and examining the distribution of the national wealth among them. It explained how, after the Civil War, the North, directed by the Republican party, seized economic control of the nation and maintained it through corporate monopoly. The result was that by 1930 the North, with 21 percent of the territory and 57 percent of the people, owned and controlled approximately 85 percent of the nation's wealth, although about 90 percent of the natural resources were located in the South and West. (I thought of that in examining the distribution of the presidents of this Association. The North has had 90 percent of the presidents and about the same proportion of nearly everything else.) The book in original form trod on the toes of a powerful monopoly of patents, and it in turn trod on my publisher, leading to expurgation in galley of all reference to this company and to its product, glass bottles. The book was quickly declared out of print on the ground that it did not sell.

But it had done its work. The Hartford Empire Company was hauled to Washington where I saw the same men who had dictated virtually what I should print about milk bottles quail before Thurmond Arnold's young attorneys who gave an examination that Hartford Empire did not pass. The book was also a factor in causing Franklin D. Roosevelt to issue the report of 1938 and his sensational letter declaring the South the economic problem Number One of the nation, and expressing the determination to do something about what he called the imbalance.

Though declared out of print, the book would not die. The federal investigation of the Hartford Empire Company put all the records in the public domain. From these records I told the whole story and published the revised book myself. It is now in the fourth edition, has sold 15,000 copies, and is still in print. The original publisher is out of business. Recently I re-examined the distribution of the national wealth among the sections to find that between 1930 and 1950 the South and West gained in every category of wealth and well-being, in some cases spectacularly; and the North, while still far in the lead, lost correspondingly. Now with the Giants and Dodgers in California, with the House led by and the Senate and this Association presided over by Texans, it would seem the North is going the way of the Republican party.

The story of my fourth adventure in history is told in *The Great Frontier*, published in 1952. It, like *The Great Plains,* is based on a single idea, best expressed in the question: What effect did all the new lands discovered by Columbus and his associates around 1500 have on Western civilization during the following 450 years? What happened to 10,000,000 people shut up in the wedge of western Eurasia when they suddenly acquired title to six times the amount of land they had before, fresh land, thinly tenanted, loaded with resources too great to be comprehended? What did all this wealth and the act of appropriating it do to and for the 10,000,000 poverty-stricken people of Western Europe and their descendants?

Slowly the thesis emerged, the boom hypothesis, around which the story was to be told. *The Great Frontier* precipitated a boom on the Metropolis, a boom of gigantic proportions which began when Columbus returned from his first

18

voyage and accelerated until all the new lands had been ap-
propriated. This boom accompanied the rise of modern civilization and attended the birth of a set of new institutions and
ideas designed to service a booming society, chief among them
modern democracy and capitalism and the idea of progress.
The small booms we know, based on oil or gold or soil, burst
when that on which they are based is depleted. They have all
been temporary, and the period in which they existed has
been considered abnormal. But this big boom, based on all
the resources of the Great Frontier, lasted so long that it was
considered normal and its institutions permanent. By about
1900 the Great Frontier, of which the American frontier was
a fragment, began to close, and as it closed the idea of progress and the efficacy of democracy and capitalism were questioned, put in strain, and since 1914 these boom-born ideas
and institutions have been fighting a defensive action. Unless
we find some means to restore the boom, future historians
may look back on the period from 1500 to 1950 as the Age
of the Great Frontier, the most abnormal period in the history of mankind. So ran the argument.

Given the point of view of a Great Frontier set over
against the Metropolis, many aspects of modern history fell
into place, could be understood rather than remembered. Under the controlling idea, or thesis, many sub-theses emerged,
such as the windfall theory of wealth, the relation of the
Great Frontier to modern romantic literature as illustrated in
Coleridge's "Rime of the Ancient Mariner," the utopias, and
such feats of imagination as *Gulliver's Travels,* Defoe's *Robinson Crusoe,* and Stevenson's *Treasure Island,* examples of
what the Great Frontier did to the human imagination.

In the realm of economics I advanced the theory of the
dual circulation of wealth, which, if true, might lead the
economists to re-examine their subject and data and their
basic assumptions. The economists have thus far treated
wealth as if it had but one motion, circulation from hand to
hand among the people. Actually, since the discoveries if not

19

before, wealth has had *two* motions. It circulates horizontally among the people, and in modern times it has moved vertically between the people and the sovereign, and the character of its vertical movement has had profound effects on modern institutions.

By the discoveries the sovereigns of Europe acquired title to all the lands of the Great Frontier. Unable to use so much land, the sovereigns began dispersing it to the people, letting it sift down in townships, leagues, and quarter sections, eventually to small people. This gigantic land dispersal went on constantly from 1600 to 1900, three booming centuries when wealth was moving vertically, from the sovereign downward to the people, making them economically independent and politically free. When the frontier closed, the sovereign had nothing more to give, and then he began the reverse process of taking, not from the frontier, but from some of the people in order to have something to give to others. In short, wealth began making a complete vertical circuit, instead of flowing in one direction. This vertical circulation today supplements the horizontal circulation so precious to free enterprisers and keeps it going. If this idea of the dual movement of wealth is true—and it seems obvious once it is pointed out—it should, I thought, have far-reaching implications for the study of modern economics.

The journey through the Great Frontier was a mental adventure of the first magnitude. Many splendid vistas opened, and many things that were familiar took on new meaning. It was lonely there; many times I did not know which way to go, and I, like the boy driving the goats, would have been glad to go home.

As I look back on this program of work, I see in the four books a record of a mental adventure into an expanding world. *The Texas Rangers* was local, simple in structure, and involved little thought. *The Great Plains* was regional, based on a single idea. *Divided We Stand* was national. *The Great Frontier* was international, and, like *The Great Plains*, was

20

the expansion of an idea. The common element in them all is the frontier, dominant in three and present in the fourth. Taken together they tell the story of the expansion of the mind from a hard-packed West Texas dooryard to the outer limits of the Western World.

When one writes of the West and the frontier, the question is sure to arise as to his relation to Frederick J. Turner. It is often said that Webb belongs to the Turner school. I would like to take this opportunity to state my relation to Turner as I see it. No one respects Turner more than I, and no one is less patient with those who take exception to some detail in Turner and argue from this small base that his thesis is wrong. There are few so foolish as to say that the existence of a vast body of free land would not have some effects on the habits, customs, and institutions of those who had access to it. That is essentially what Turner said in his essay about the United States, and that is what I said in *The Great Frontier* about western European civilization. Though my canvas was bigger than Turner's, and my span of time a century longer, the thesis is the same. Turner looked at a fragment of the frontier; I tried to look at the whole thing. If Turner's thesis is true, then mine is true; if his is a fallacy, then mine is also fallacious. Since Turner was first in time and I a generation later, I will probably always be counted as a part of the Turner school. And I accept this as an honor.

The question that may arise is this: Am I in the frontier school because Turner led me there or because I stumbled into it independently? I think I stumbled in. I cannot prove this, but I would like to submit evidence of my assumption.

As already stated, I never had a course in western history. I never saw Turner. At the time I began writing *The Great Plains,* I had never read the Turner essay, and I refrained from reading it until I had completed the study. There is little in Turner's writing to suggest that he anticipated the idea developed in *The Great Plains.* The frontier that he knew was east of the Mississippi.

21

If I did not follow Turner, whom did I follow? What is my intellectual heritage? You will recall that I have paid repeated tribute to Lindley Miller Keasbey, the talented professor of the nonexistent field of institutional history. It was Keasbey who gave me an understanding for and appreciation of the relationship between an environment and the civilization resting upon it; it was Keasbey who taught me, and many others, to begin with the geology or geography, and build upon this foundation the superstructure of the flora, fauna, and anthropology, arriving at last at the modern civilization growing out of this foundation. Turner did not proceed in that manner, but that is the way I proceeded in *The Great Plains* and less obviously in *The Great Frontier*.

But who is Keasbey? To answer that question, we must go back to the European thinkers who influenced Turner and Keasbey. Prominent among them was an Italian economist, sociologist, and philosopher named Achille Loria (1857–1943) who wrote in the last quarter of the nineteenth century. Loria's name is found in the Turner literature, and Turner quoted him in the 1893 essay.[2]

As an indication that Turner might have found some comfort in the Italian, I quote the following from Loria: "A tyranny . . . is . . . automatically regulated by the existence of free land, which of itself renders the exercise of true despotic government impossible so long as slavery is unheard of; for the subjects always have a way of avoiding oppression of the sovereign by abandoning him and setting up for themselves upon an unoccupied territory."[3] The occasional reference to Loria in the literature caused me to look him up in the library. Imagine my surprise when I found that the English translation of one of Loria's most important books was done by Lindley Miller Keasbey of institutional history. If Loria influenced Turner, he most certainly influenced Keasbey, who influenced me more than any other man. If this is my line of descent, then I am on a collateral line from the European scholars through Keasbey rather than from those scholars by way of Turner.

A book dealing with an idea and its ramifications, with a thesis or interpretation, is more likely to be kicked around by the critics than one that sticks to the facts, and this may explain why nonventuresome historians, schooled in intellectual timidity, are so factual. Both *The Great Plains* and *The Great Frontier* are idea books, and each has received its share of critical attention. This is to be expected and as it should be. If an idea or interpretation cannot survive a critic, any critic, it is no good anyway. If the idea is sound, then the criticism advertises and spreads it. William E. Dodd told us once never to reply to a critic, and I have never voluntarily done so. The critic is entitled to his view, and the author will waste his time trying to change it. The idea has its own destiny, and once launched, it is independent of both author and critic.

In conclusion, I want to pay tribute to a group not accustomed to receiving it. I refer to several generations of graduate students who have generously contributed their time, effort, and ingenuity in working out the details and ramifications of ideas presented to them in seminar. I have no notion of what they got from me, but I do know that I got a great deal from them, and they a great deal from one another.

They were good companions on some exciting intellectual excursions into the Great Plains and into the vastly greater frontier. Some of them will have their own story to tell, and I trust they will have the courage to tell it as they see it, and never as they think I might want it told. I would rather liberate than bind them.

This exercise tonight comes at the end of my academic service. This address is the last act of an official character that I expect to perform, a sort of climax to a high adventure. Because my performance can bring no rewards and inflict no penalties, I have said what I wanted to say in the way I wanted to say it.

If what I have said is unorthodox, it is consistent with much that I have done. I do not recommend my course to others, but it seems in retrospect almost inevitable for me.

III   The STORY of some PRAIRIE INVENTIONS

WHEN I was asked to speak to the Nebraska Historical Society on the occasion of its seventy-fifth anniversary celebration, they conferred on me an honor of which I am both conscious and proud, and an obligation which requires all I have to fulfill. It is true that I have had some experience in directing an organization such as this, the Texas State Historical Association which is about twenty years younger than yours. I think I know something of the problems that confront a director, and I know something also of the pleasure derived from bringing together those few who devote their time and energy to preserving the fading records and legends of the past.

Those of us who devote ourselves to state or county or community history are sometimes made to feel that the work lacks the significance that attaches to more ambitious undertakings. I do not hold that view because I know that all history is local. All places are local to the people thereabout, and only the consequences of what took place give what happened there importance.

I did not come here to tell you about the battles and the bloodshed you have had in Nebraska. You have been fortunate in having few battles and little organized bloodshed within your state, and I trust that your good fortune endures.

But a battle of great consequence has been fought here in Nebraska and in neighboring states. It seems appropriate that I talk of this battle—of things which your people and my people worked out in the great laboratory of hazardous living. I want to give examples from the approximate date of the organization of this Society. It so happens that in the period from about 1870 to 1900 the common people of this whole region in which you live were conducting in patient silence one of the greatest experiments in living that has ever occurred in this broad land. They were fighting a desperate battle for life and survival, conducting it against great odds, and they were doing it without guns and often with very little butter. In this battle everybody was a private and each his own general. There were no such heroes as Robert E. Lee or Abraham Lincoln. There were no parades, no flags, and no music. There were no hospitals for the casualties. There are no cemeteries set aside for those who perished in that conflict, and on Decoration Day the graves of these unknown soldiers—men, women and children—are in the main unmarked and never decorated by patriotic organizations.

You must be wondering why you have not heard more of this battle. You have heard more of it than you think, but you may not have noticed it because it was, and it still is, a part of your life. You here in Nebraska are still engaged, as are we in Texas, in Kansas, in the Dakotas, throughout all these western states. If the conflict is less fierce now than it was around 1878, '88, '98, it is because we are the beneficiaries of the victories won by those first campaigners who tackled the enemy almost with bare hands.

26

I come tonight to talk to you of some things these soldiers of the plains left by the "wheel scarr'd road." I talk of those who fought the plain and the prairie wherein you dwell.

What then is this battle of which I speak? It was in essence the battle of all the people with a land which to them was new and strange. It was the struggle of a people, who in all their history had never lived in this kind of country, learning to live in this kind of country. And what kind of country is this, and why was it so strange to the early Nebraskan? When your Society was organized in 1878 I daresay that not a charter member of it was born in Nebraska, and few of them in a country in any way similar to Nebraska. They were from another land. They had come out of the East, from a land of tall trees, bubbling springs, running rivers, and practically no grass. For generations their fathers had lived in the forest and had seen the morning and evening sun only through the tracery of the forest's rich green foliage. Those people literally dug their farms out of the woods, and from the ruins of the woods they made what they needed—their cabins, fences, cribs, churns, beds, beehives, horse troughs, baby cradles, and gate hinges. These early Nebraskans were a forest people, and their whole life and their whole way of living had been geared into and articulated with the forests which lay behind them. In that forest their work was hard, but they knew how to perform it. There were few mysteries and unknown quantities in the problems of living. Their civilization stood firmly on three legs—land, water and timber.

It was about the middle of the century and later when these forest dwellers came out of the woods. They left the shade and the comfort and the certainty of a known life and stood appalled in the mighty presence of this strange land, a land without timber, with rarely enough water, a hemisphere of grass with a flat and level floor beneath and an inverted bowl of limitless sky above. They had never seen so far or so little as in this land of vast immensity. It was as if they were

27

on the sea, but they were on the plain.

The plain has moods like the sea . . .
The plain grows dark; like the sea
It holds no shelter.

Of the plains John J. Ingalls said: "Above their receding horizons forever broods a pathetic solemnity, born of distance, silence and solitude." In the same kind of country Hamlin Garland described the sunrise:

The sun up-sprang,
Its light swept the plain like a sea
Of golden water, and the blue-gray dome
That soared above the settler's shack
Was lighted to magical splendor.

But these early comers to Nebraska had too many hard tasks before them to dwell long under the spell of the magical splendor created by sunrise of a wet morning on the green and undulating sea of the plain. These early comers were baffled and often beaten by the unsolved problems of the plains. In a land where a furrow could be plowed a hundred miles long, they had no plow that would turn the prairie sod, no rails with which to build their accustomed fences, no logs with which to construct the classic American cabin, no weapons with which to meet the mounted Indians, and they were always short of water.

Their civilization had stood on three legs—land, water, and timber; here two of these legs were knocked out, and they stood on the single leg of land. It is no wonder that they sometimes toppled over in failure. The remarkable thing is the manner in which they worked out their problems and made the radical changes that enable them—some of them— to stay in the country that we now hold so dear.

In speaking of this Battle of the Plains, I would not have you think that I speak of Nebraska alone. That battlefield was half as big as the nation. It stretched from Mexico on the south to Canada on the north; it was several hundred miles wide, extending from the edge of the eastern woodland into and through the Rocky Mountains. All along the eastern edge of this land thousands of people were engaged in a common struggle. Fortunately, an occasional victory in any part of the country—in Illinois, Kansas, Texas or Nebraska—conferred its benefits on plainsmen elsewhere. The problem of one was the problem of all, and the fruits of success in one place were soon enjoyed in other places.

We need a symbol for the spirit of these people, for these successes, these far-reaching victories. I could find no symbol more fitting than the windmills which by 1878 began to rear their wheels on the far horizons, signaling to man that here was his most precious treasure, cool clear water. The windmill was like a flag marking the spot where a small victory had been won in the fight for water in an arid land. The windmill threw in with nature and capitalized on the least expensive plains commodity—the wind—to produce the scarcest and most valuable commodity—water—at the least possible expense. Life was always tolerable, and often comfortable, as long as the old windmill kept a-turning. The wheel bears some resemblance to a giant sunflower, and it turns into the wind of its own volition as the sunflower turns into the sun. It was as dependable as the wind, and the wind of the plains is more dependable than the rain.

This symbol of the windmill is appropriate here because Nebraska was the very *heart* of the windmill country. Its development was carried out with greater ingenuity here in Nebraska than in any other state I know. And finally, it was a Nebraska citizen and scholar who saw something of interest and importance in what the farmers and ranchmen along the Platte, the Republican, and the Loup were doing with windmills, and he took the time to make the record of which I shall speak later.

I must remind you again that I am dealing with the changes men were compelled to make when they passed from the woodland of the East into the open plain of the West.

I shall deal with the problems incidental to that passage. I shall illustrate with several examples, selected from different plains and prairie states. I deal with a period of about one generation, say from 1840 to 1900, the period in which a woodland people made the passage and learned to live on the plains. The first example has to do with guns, the second with fences, a third with plows, and the last with windmills. What the people had to learn when they came to the plains were new ways of fighting, of fencing, of farming, and of providing water.

I have on this table a long rifle and a Colt revolver, a piece of barbed wire, and a disc plow. These are simple things, but they are highly significant, and each is related to the adaptations that people made when they left the forest to live in this open country.

The first thing the American people had to learn when they came out on the plains was to stand up to the enemies they found there. These were Indians but quite different from any that the settlers had contended with before. These were Plains Indians, wild, nomadic, fierce and unconquerable. Such were the Comanche, Apache, Cheyenne, Blackfoot, and several others. What was more important, these were horse Indians, and they had developed a technique of fighting on horseback. The American had never had to fight Indians on horseback before because the woodland Indians were pedestrians. The Americans had no weapons suited to fighting on horseback, especially in the Indian style. They had the long rifle, sometimes known as the Kentucky or Tennessee rifle. A specimen of this weapon I have here, and I think you can see without further elaboration that it was designed for a man who had both feet planted on the ground. The Indian carried from twenty to thirty arrows, and he could shoot them so rapidly from a running horse that he could keep one in the air all the time. The American with this long rifle had but one shot, and when that was spent it took him a long time to reload this cap-and-ball rifle. In this interval he was quite helpless while the Indian was in full command of the situation. It is clear that the American needed a weapon that could be used on horseback, that carried more than a single shot.

The need for this weapon was first felt most keenly in Texas, most keenly there because the Texans were among the first to venture living in the edge of the land where the Comanche raided and ravaged the settlements on horseback. The man who provided the gun for the plainsman, for the horseman, was Samuel Colt. He invented a multiple shot revolving pistol carrying five or six shots about 1830, began manufacturing it in 1832 at about the time the Texans were developing their bitter conflict with the mounted Indians. Colt had no idea of creating a weapon just for Texans but thought he had made one suited for the military men of the United States. In this he was at first disappointed. The army condemned his weapon. The people of the United States were not yet much in contact with the Plains Indian, had not become horsemen, and would not buy the guns. By accident some of them found their way to the Republic of Texas and into the hands of a small group of Texas Rangers stationed on the border to guard against the incursions of the mounted Comanches. The Texas Rangers under Jack Hays tried the revolvers first in the Indian battle of the Pedernales, the first battle in which the Americans fought Plains Indians on horseback. But the little Republic and the people of Texas were too poor to buy many of Colt's guns, and nobody else would buy them at all. The result was that Samuel Colt went into bankruptcy in 1842. The Mexican War broke out in 1846, and immediately the Texas Rangers enlisted under Colonel John Coffee (Jack) Hays. Hays and a few of his men still had the multiple shot pistols, but the rank and file had none. The rank and file demanded revolvers and were so insistent that an order went up to Washington for one thousand revolvers, two for each of the five hundred Texas Rangers. Colt had been in bankruptcy for four years, had got rid of all his weapons, and had no money to make more. When the government finally found him, he was dressed in a long black coat and a tall top hat, standing on the back end of a medicine wagon selling nostrums to the public. He was pulled off the wagon by the Indian fighters of the plains who had reached from the deserts of Texas into the verdant land of New England to rescue Samuel Colt from obscurity, to make him rich, and to make him famous throughout the open country where cowboys and peace officers rode horseback in their daily work. The men on horseback—cattlemen, cowboys, peace officers, and the American cavalry—took over the open country to subdue the Indians. They took the country but held it briefly because the farmers were beating hard at the eastern gate. The farmers had already pushed into the eastern edge of the plains, into the fertile prairie land, but they were stopped because they had nothing with which to fence their crops from the cattle, their own cattle and their neighbors'. Farming was impossible without fences, and the prairiemen, having outrun the forest and the rocks, had nothing with which to make a rail fence or a stone wall, and they knew no other fence.

Along the edge of the open country, of which eastern Nebraska is a part, men began experimenting with every conceivable substitute that could be converted into an economical fence—one they could afford to build, a fence without rails and without rocks. They tried hedges made of rose bushes, mesquite, prickly pear, and finally of Osage orange, an indigenous, thorny, stubborn, and hardy plant. Nurserymen handled the plants, and Osage orange seeds sold for five dollars a pound or fifty dollars a bushel. You still have survivals of these hedges on your prairies, reminders of the efforts of your fathers to make a fence for a treeless land. What men learned from the use of hedges was that you had to have thorns to turn cattle, and the idea of a thorny fence was basic in the solution of the fence problem by western farmers.

Three New England farmers who had moved to the

prairies of Illinois took the idea of the thorn and converted it into a fence that was cheap enough and effective enough to meet the needs of a treeless land. On the thorn they made a barb—more barbaric than the thorn. They made barbed wire, and they first called such a fence a thorn wire fence.

The invention did not come out of a formal laboratory, yet it came out of the great frontier laboratory where thousands of little men were fighting the Battle of the Plains. We see them stumbling from one thing to another, trying this, trying that, and finally these God-fearing transplanted New Englanders with keen noses for the main chance stumbled upon the solution so essential to the treeless half of the continent.

The three men were Joseph Glidden, Jacob Haisch, and Isaac Ellwood—and you can tell by their names—Joseph, Jacob, and Isaac—that they had background. It was only after they made fortunes that they became converted sinners.

The story of how they got the idea of a barbed wire cannot be known with accuracy because these farmers did not make written records. But after they got rich, they began suing one another, hired lawyers who were able to prove almost anything in court, and we have sworn testimony for whatever it is worth. I will not confuse you with that.

A man named Rose conceived the idea of making a cheap fence by using strips of wood studded with nail points. These strips he attached to posts with the sharp nails facing the stock. About 1872 he exhibited this device at a county fair at DeKalb, Illinois, and all the curious and jealous farmers came to examine it to see if it was practical. Among them were Joseph Glidden, Jacob Haisch, and Isaac Ellwood. It was later claimed that all got the idea of a thorn fence from the Rose exhibit. All we know for certain is that within a year all three men were making some form of barbed wire.

Glidden says that he got the idea because his wife was pestering him to keep the dogs out of her flower beds where they went on hot days to scratch out a cool place to lie down.

He says he put a smooth wire around the beds, and then tried putting rude barbs on it. But the barbs would slide laterally or would turn on the smooth wire and were not effective. You have noticed that all barbed wire is made of two strands twisted. You would think anyone would know that the way to make barbed wire is to twist two strands, but this simple thing had to be learned. I may say that the twisting is essential and makes the wire a sort of spring which contracts and expands with heat and cold. Only twisted wire will stay tight in all weather. The twisting serves the further purpose of holding the barbs in place and keeping them from rotating. Glidden says that he learned about this twisting by accident. He picked up some tangled smooth wire, and in a flash it occurred to him that twisting would be a good idea. He fastened two wires to the shaft of a grindstone and called his wife to turn the crank while he held the wires. He had a hired man named Andrew Johnson who told about the first barbs. He said that at night, after the day's work was done, they made the first barbs. They used an old wall coffee mill for this purpose. In the shaft of the coffee mill they fixed two pins, one in the center, one off-center. They inserted a wire between the pins and gave the crank a complete turn to form a circle. Then they cut the wire to finish the barb. With a bucket full of barbs a boy would climb a windmill tower and thread the barbs on strands of greased wire. The barbs would be spaced and set by a hammer blow and then the two strands, one with barbs, and one without, would be twisted to hold the barbs in place. They sold the wire as fast as they could make it—at twenty cents a pound. All this happened in the year 1873, five years before this Society was formed. By the time this Society was formed, Joseph, Jacob, and Isaac were all rich; the United States Steel Corporation took over the making of barbed wire, and all of Nebraska and all of the Great Plains country were going under fence. The farmer could see his homestead, and the cattleman could, for the first time, fence his twenty—or sixty—section ranch.

34

But even with the invention of a practical and economical fence, the Battle of the Plains was not won. When these farmers came out on the plains they had no plow that would turn the prairie sod. The plow they brought from the eastern woodland, from the red hills of Georgia and the rocky lands of Vermont and Massachusetts may best be described as a dirt pusher. It had a blunt point and a flat wing or share that did not turn but simply pushed the loose earth over towards the previous furrow. Now the prairie and plains earth was not loose. It was fertile and hard, and it was bound together in a tight mass by millions of grass roots. To plow it was like plowing a Brussels carpet six inches thick. No dirt pusher could even stay in the ground. The matted sod of the plains could not be pushed. It had to be cut by a long sharp point, a long point carried back to the long, bent share, and finally this ribbon of matted earth, flowing in large blocks from the plains plow, had to be turned upside down into the previous furrow.

I wish that the invention of this plains plow had brought on the lawsuits that barbed wire brought so that the lawyers could have got some perjured testimony for the historians to use as an original source. The real story of this innovation in plows lies in the graves of the prairie blacksmiths who stood over their forges to hammer out the points and shares that would turn the matted soil of the plains upside down. It would, I am sure, be the same old story of stumbling, experimenting by hundreds of blacksmiths and thousands of farmers until the shape and the character of the plow were discovered, accepted, and perfected. Once it became perfected the big farms unrolled like black rugs laid in fields of green or brown grass.

Second to the turning plow was the disc which became so important in cultivating the expanding fields of the West. It was my good fortune to get on the trail of how the disc plow was invented, to find the son of the blacksmith who made it, and even to find his original disc plow with the anvil and hammer marks on it. It is here for you to see, one of the most valuable artifacts left from the Battle of the Plains. I shall relate the story as I have been able to piece it together.

I was conducting a contest in local history, offering prizes to the high school student who wrote the best essay on his local community. One of these essays came in from the prairie town of Clifton, Texas. It was about a Swedish settler named Ole Ringness who was a leader in his community. He was also a blacksmith. A letter came one day from far-off Sweden saying that another contingent of immigrants was coming to Texas. They would land at Galveston, and they wanted some of their friends to meet the boat. Ole Ringness was selected to drive to Galveston and conduct the party to their new home. It was summer time. The drought was on as it often is in western Texas and western Nebraska. Ole's wagon was good, but the tires had become loose in the drought, and he had shrunk them so much that one wheel, a front wheel no doubt, had become badly dished. To say that a wheel is dished means that it has taken the form of a large plate or soup bowl. Naturally, Ole Ringness kept an eye on that bad wheel, and he noticed that as it unrolled the dreary miles, it threw the earth aside, making a furrow behind. Now when one drives a wagon and team two hundred miles, he has a great deal of time to think. Ole Ringness did a lot of thinking. Would it be possible, he asked himself, to make a plow out of a dished wheel? And would it not also be possible to set a series of these dished wheels on a common axle and break a strip of land two feet or ten feet wide instead of six or eight inches as was the case with the steel turning plow. I am sure that Ole Ringness was a poor host to the new immigrants on the long drive back home, for his thoughts were on the original idea he had. He could hardly wait to get back to his shop, fire up his forge, and hammer out his revolutionary idea. At any rate, that is what he did, and here is the dished wheel, the very disc that he made. We found it on his little farm and got permission from his son to place it in the museum at The University of Texas where I trust it will be

36

appreciated. As you look at this rude disc, at the hammer marks, I would like for you to remember that it represents the dream of a soldier in this Battle of the Plains.

For the inventor it was an empty dream. The story says that he decided to go to Washington to get a patent so that the lawsuits could begin. He went to Washington by way of New York, and while in New York he took sick and died. His invention was never patented. It may not have been the first disc plow, but it was original, and it does illustrate the drama and the tragedy of the battle I am describing.

My last illustration is a Nebraska story, and it happens to be well documented. The windmill was not invented in Nebraska, or for that matter in the United States. But we did have in Nebraska, as I have said, one of the most interesting developments of the windmill that I know of anywhere. The story begins with the good wet years that made the Plains so attractive in the 1880's. In these wet years the farmers made their great invasion of the semiarid country to the west of Lincoln. They took up homesteads along the Platte, on both sides, and in the other valleys. But the lean, dry years followed the fat, wet ones, and from 1886 far into the nineties, the settlers were driven back to the green country. Your novelists, poets, and historians have told the story of their retreat, and I shall not repeat it. But not all retreated. Some held their ground either because they were unable to move or because they had found a way to live with the country. Our story concerns those who stayed, those who held on until the rains came again. It particularly concerns those who stayed because of the windmill to which they clung—life preserver in a sea of aridity.

These windmills of Nebraska were not those factory-made rosettes which you still see whirling so lightly on your western horizon. Few of those people had money enough to buy a windmill. Just as the people had to learn to make fences without rails, so they had to learn to make windmills without steel and without money. And there sprang up from Lincoln to the western edge of Nebraska and on into Colorado on both sides of the Platte Valley the greatest aggregation of homemade windmills known in all history. The Platte was a ribbon of sand, and the only supply of water was far below the surface.

You had here in Lincoln a professor Erwin Hinckley Barbour who held the office of state geologist. He became interested in homemade windmills. He said:[1]

> Nebraska seems to be the heart and the center of the windmill movement. The famous Platte Valley, with its broad expanse and shallow wells, is a veritable windmill arena. From Omaha west through the State, a distance of 500 miles, and even beyond to Denver, there is a constant succession of these creations of a sturdy population.

In the summer of 1897 Professor Barbour employed three University students, equipped them with teams, saddle horses, camp wagons, cameras, and camp equipment. He sent them from Lincoln to Denver south of the Platte and had them return north to the river. They went to study homemade windmills. They photographed them and made records of their makers and owners. Said Professor Barbour: "They found these unique and interesting windmills everywhere. Going over the same ground in person the following year, eight to ten mills were commonly found clustered about a town, each widely separated town having a dominant . . . type . . . They are also found in the Republican Valley and the valleys of the Loup rivers and their tributaries."

Professor Barbour found that the windmills fell into about seven main classifications and that they varied within each class. There were twenty varieties listed in all.

The main classes were Jumbo or Paddle Wheel or Go-devil, Merry-go-round, Battle Ax, Holland, and Turbines. Time does not permit me to describe them, and Dr. Olson did not rise to my challenge to find a single survivor of these homemade mills to exhibit here. I doubt that a single one does exist.

What recommended these mills was their low cost. Of the Jumbo, Professor Barbour wrote: "The Jumbos are not wholly ornamental, but that is unimportant. The Jumbo has served useful purposes in hundreds of frontier homes . . . The average cost of such mills is $4." J. L. Brown, nurseryman near Kearney, had one he used for irrigation of garden, strawberry patch, and fruit trees that cost $1.50. Professor Barbour said:

"The four-blade battle ax . . . is the favorite type around Grand Island and farther west. Such a mill, with pumping capacity for 100 to 125 head of cattle, may cost $2 or $3, but should not cost $10, and may be built by those who are inventive without any outlay. Poles and strong limbs (for the tower) answer the purpose as well as new lumber, old dry-goods boxes furnish materials suitable for fans, old wire, nails, and bolts are common on every farm. . . . In most of them (battle-axes) journals, gearings, rods, springs, wheels, nuts, bolts, braces, and lumber of discarded machinery are used."

Of the service these homemade mills rendered, we have this from Professor Barbour:

1. The contrast between the Nebraska farm without a windmill and one with: "one with cattle crowding around the well, waiting for some thoughtless farm hand to pump them their scanty allowance of water, the other where the cattle are grazing and the tanks and troughs are full and running over."

2. It made the difference in time of drought between the family who was able to hold on and the one that had to give up. The irrigation of one acre from a homemade windmill often produced more than all the rest of the farm or ranch.

3. It provided something in the way of luxury: running water in the house, green lawns in a desert, shade trees around a school house set on a bleak hilltop. There was always hope as long as the windmill kept turning.

And so we end with the symbol with which we set out.

39

Behind the struggle of these people, behind the search for a horseman's weapon, a plains fence, and a prairie plow, and the effort to provide water by use of the wind—behind all these it was the spirit of the people, the common people, that kept on a-turning. And like the windmill it seemed to operate best when facing the high winds of hardship and adversity.

IV PHYSICS, HISTORY, and FATE

AS I examined the program of the February, 1954, meeting of the American Physical Society I was struck by the exclusive concern of the members with what may be called immediacy. The papers seem to deal primarily with problems now in the process of solution. Nowhere did I find that the physicists are concerned with perspective, past or future, with where their subject came from or whither it is going. The practicing physicists seem little concerned with the relation of their subject to the world that lies around it.

I shall attempt here to place the subject of physics in its historical context, to show that it arose under peculiar historical conditions, that it grew to its present importance under conditions singularly favorable to it, that those happy conditions are now being modified, and that physics in the future may find the going much harder than it has been during its whole history as a science.

It is not strange that physics has thus far disregarded its own history, and that of civilization itself, because it has been too busy making history and shaping the civilization. The first contributions of physics were wholly favorable to mankind. As long as physics worked in constructive ways—as it did for a considerable time—the men who set its forces in motion could go about their business, tend their laboratories and not worry about consequences so beneficial. But when the consequences began to threaten the welfare, and even the existence of civilization, the physicists can no longer be indifferent. When, however, they seek a broader view, trying to see the relationship of what they have done and will do to all that is around them, to civilization itself, they become historians, and they enter into a realm quite different in both its intent and method from the one in which they have been accustomed to operate.

In approaching physics historically, it is necessary to state the historian's function and his method. His function is to view society—dispassionately if he can—and explain its past actions with as much reason and as little passion as possible. He is, as distinguished from the physicist, severely handicapped in his method. His handicap is that he must seek truth without benefit of laboratory. Since he has no laboratory, can in the nature of his material have none, has no possible way of demonstrating by experiment, the historian can never prove anything in the sense that the physicist can. The historian does collect evidence, usually in the form of records of what happened, but he can never prove that the records are infallible or that he has all the pertinent evidence. Furthermore, he can never divest himself of his own point of view. For these reasons the historian's conclusions are always tentative, never universally accepted, and are almost certain to be discarded partially or totally by his successors. This whole procedure must seem highly unsatisfactory—and unscientific, as indeed it is—but the historian has no choice but to use it. For him there is no other method.

What the historian does as he peers into the kaleido-scopic past is this: he tries to see relationships among the varied past activities of man. He searches for connections, appraises forces and treats them as causes operating to produce resultant effects. If the historian looks at the shifting scene long enough—never directly but through other men's records—he begins to see patterns forming; a sort of crystal-lization seems to occur as the lens of his mind takes focus. Though these may be lovely patterns, they are more intan-gible than the stuff physicists deal with. The patterns can never be touched or tested by the senses; they can only be described as they appear to the informed and questing mind. Since the historian must depend on the skill of his descrip-tion, the clarity of his exposition, he must give more attention to the art of presentation than his scientist brother needs to give. If he is less of a scientist, he may be more of an artist.

Once the patterns form, the historian begins to seek out the one pattern for special attention, usually the one that seems to him to dominate the age he is trying to understand. This pattern takes on importance for him; he is likely to think that he has discovered some force or influence that controlled some things, that seemed to touch and color everything in the society that it accompanies.

At this stage the historian is likely to become excited, if not slightly possessed, at the prospect. If he be daring enough, and disregardful enough of his reputation for safe mediocrity, he does what the real scientist does: he sets up a working hypothesis which holds that a certain ingredient of history, the factor that concerns him, has helped to shape mankind's action and helped direct history throughout the period of its presence. Having formulated the hypothesis, the historian hunts all available evidence to support it, refute it, or modify it. If the evidence does in general support the hypothesis, if nothing is found to refute it, the hypothesis is launched as a thesis in a book or an article for the critical appraisal of col-leagues and the scholarly world.

It would be a great comfort to the historian if he could bolster his case with a record of controlled experimental demonstrations all of which point to his major conclusions. This he can never do; he must always submit his case to the court on circumstantial evidence. It is not often that a scientist launches a thesis that he has not proved, that he has not demonstrated in the laboratory, that he has not supported by figures as convincing as the multiplication table. It may be suggested, however, that there are exceptions, and notable among them are Charles Darwin and Albert Einstein.

The question arises as to how a thesis supported by circumstantial evidence ever achieves validity. *How* does the high court decide whether the interpreter has made his case? *When* does the court decide? The last question as to *when* is easiest answered. There is rarely, if ever, a quick decision. The court—which is the public—ponders the case a long time, often engages in acrimonious argument and the best the historian ever gets is a split decision.

The thesis or interpretation can eventually find a measure of acceptance by meeting certain tests. The chief test is whether the explanation offered gives *meaning* to the past, whether it proves useful in enabling others to see some order in the welter of facts and conflicting opinions. If it does establish a sort of intellectual life line, a control point from which the mind may take off and to which it may return, the hypothesis is likely to find wide acceptance. If things fit into the explanation, fall into place like blocks in a puzzle, and if there are not too many blocks left over, the thoughtful reader will say: "This stuff makes sense to me." If it makes enough sense to enough readers, then in time the work may be referred to as standard, a classic. This is what has happened to the theses of Adam Smith, William Graham Sumner, and Charles Darwin. We still do not know that the histories written by these men are correct, but what they wrote has been so useful, so illuminating and so suggestive that they are still spoken of with great respect. They have achieved a practical validity, but by a process much slower and more tentative than is often the case in demonstrable science.

The method of investigation described above is one I followed in launching some months ago the thesis of the Great Frontier. The high court is now wrangling mildly over it, and only time—about twenty years—will tell as to its fate. Naturally I think the thesis has validity in that it explains some things about the modern world better than other interpretations. Naturally I would have to hold this opinion to justify the years spent in elaborating the idea and tracing out the pattern of the Great Frontier.[1] My view of physics and other modern sciences is that which one gets when these subjects are viewed from the vantage point of the Great Frontier.

The thesis advanced is that one of the powerful forces operating on western civilization since 1500 has been the Great Frontier. And the Great Frontier is identified as all the new lands of the western world discovered by Columbus and his associates around 1500. It comprised North and South America, Australia, a large part of Africa, and thousands of islands scattered over the oceans. In a brief span of time the discoverers brought these continents and these islands and laid them as a free gift in the lap of impoverished and crowded Europe. As a physicist might view it, they brought a new element, a strong ingredient of gigantic proportions, a new force of immense power and strength, and suddenly injected it into the society of western civilization. These new lands—the Great Frontier comprising half of the earth—consisted of a vast body of real estate and wealth of all descriptions, lands thinly occupied by primitive peoples whose claims were lightly regarded. In effect, these continents and this wealth became the property of the nations of western Europe in an historical instant.

As a result of the injection of such an ingredient, there occurred a tremendous shift in the historical currents. Before the injection, the main forces of western history lay *within* Europe. After the injection Europe was but one factor while another of equal potency and quite different character lay outside in the Great Frontier. These were two poles of a new, enlarged, and electric field. The drama of western history from then until now—for four and one-half centuries—has been in the interaction between these two poles and the culture we know today is largely the product of that interaction.

Let us change the figure of speech and represent modern history as a tapestry woven in a continental frame, the continent of Europe on the right and the Great Frontier on the left. The interaction is like the shuttle going to and fro down the centuries—in migration, trade, commerce and war—weaving fantastic patterns of man's activities over a vast area and a long period of time. In the varied patterns of that tapestry we see blended the elements of the Metropolis of Europe and elements of the Great Frontier, the warp and woof of modern western culture.

Against the background of the tapestry woven of these components, we see modern man devising institutions, ideas, and practices suitable to the new situation, such institutions as capitalism and democracy, the novel idea of progress, the practices of rampant individualism and the marvelous unfolding of a romantic literature to glorify through the imagination all that was going on. We also can see, if we look for it, the rise of most unusual opportunities for the rapid development of pure and applied science. It is the situation existing in this age that gave physics and chemistry their big chance to become profitable and practical arts.

This age of the Great Frontier, extending from 1500 to 1950, falls into two divisions. The first may be called the Age of the Open Frontier, a long period lasting from 1500 to about 1900. The second, the one we are now in, may be called the period of the *closing* frontier, a mere introduction to a longer period that lies before us, the Age of the Closed Frontier. Since we are now only in its beginning, we cannot with any confidence foretell what the Age of the Closed Frontier will bring. But there is one thing of which we can be

46

quite sure: the Age of the Closed Frontier will be very unlike what we have known in modern times. We are now in revolution in the western world, a revolution marking the transition from the Age of the Open Frontier to that of the Closed Frontier. In retrospect this revolution may appear as our fumbling attempts to adjust our lives and institutions to the imperatives of a frontierless society.

Let us turn now to consider the first and longer period when the frontier was open. We like to say that it was dynamic, capitalistic, and democratic. Each of these features of the modern age can be related to the Great Frontier.

A dynamic society is one that is moving, going places, and doing things. Of such a society we say—and the term is quite modern—that it is making progress. Physics teaches that dynamism or a current sets up in the physical world when for any reason there is an imbalance. Who will doubt that the sudden injection of the Great Frontier into the fairly stabilized society of western Europe created just such an imbalance, destroyed equilibrium, and set in motion currents of adjustment which made the society dynamic? A clear example of this imbalance may be found in the upset land-man ratio. Late medieval Europe had a fairly stabilized ratio of about 26 persons per square mile. Then came the Great Frontier, making available more than twenty million square miles of land occupied by very few people. The old equilibrium was destroyed, and the currents of migration began to flow from Europe to the new lands to restore the balance and this flow, unchecked until after World War I, created a dynamic situation.

A second imbalance set a current of a different character flowing in the opposite direction. The Great Frontier was a land of vast resources much desired by those who remained in Europe. So, as the surplus people went out to the Great Frontier the wealth of that fabulous land began to flow back on Europe, and the stream mounted continuously until all Europe—and especially those portions which had access to the new lands—was inundated with prosperity. In the general ferment the philosophers advanced the idea of progress and new classes arose to overturn old governments and set up new ones more in harmony with the needs of a dynamic and thriving society.

As for capitalism, it comes easy when both men and wealth have such high mobility. Capitalism is an acquisitive game played by men who are free to act. The game was possible because the potential wealth was so abundant and because the real wealth was increasing faster than the population was growing. The game of playing for profit was interesting, exciting and rewarding. The circumstance of vast potential wealth in one place and many poor but eager people in another justified the coming and going and made possible the return of enough successful winners to keep the tables full. There was, temporarily, sufficient potential wealth in the Great Frontier for everybody to play at getting some of it.

The rise of capitalism was further stimulated by the introduction of frontier gold and silver in quantities unknown before. The first act of the Europeans was to tap the gold and silver storehouses of the New World. From 1500 to 1650 the precious metals poured into Europe, not by the ship load but by the fleet load. Whole armadas were used by the Spaniards to transport it. This flood of gold and silver upset the ratio existing between the amount of money and the number of people to share it, between the amount of money and the quantity of goods available. The result was a price revolution based on metals comparable to the one we have had in the last generation based on paper. In the ups and downs of that revolution, according to John Maynard Keynes, modern capitalism was born.

The overall effect of the advent of the Great Frontier may be summed up by saying that the sudden injection of excess land, excess wealth, excess gold and silver into an acquisitive society created a general boom of gigantic proportions and long duration. The boom lasted so long that we have come to think of it as the normal state, but in reality it was—as all booms are—abnormal. The frontier kept it going for four centuries because it kept the currents of wealth pouring back on the acquisitive and eager society. In this boom men came to believe they had hit the high road to eternal progress and ever increasing prosperity. In the exceptional circumstances and excitement the laws relaxed, the old restraints fell away, and the individual as the principal actor attained an importance he had rarely known before and may not know again. Democracy was born, became the favorite form of political organization, and made its way steadily against all other forms. The accelerating wealth was sufficient to pay for any mistakes, to permit laxity in government, and to provide broad tolerance for human frailty. All deficits were made up by cutting the Great Frontier up into shares and selling the stock on a rising market. Our present economic, political and social institutions formed themselves in and around the boom and served well that which nourished them. There, in a paragraph, is the overall view of this dynamic western society during the long period when the frontier was open, say from 1500 to 1900 or 1914.

It was in this booming period that the art of physics had its origin and its first opportunity to serve mankind in practical ways. That booming world so full of the stuff that physics works with was an ideal world, made to order with a high premium on what physics had to offer. That world was a physicist's paradise. So much for the rise.

During this abnormal period of expansion and boom two assumptions, both false, came to be accepted as truth. The first was that there would always be a frontier, that it was permanent and not temporal. The corollary to this was that the sources of wealth were also unlimited, and that all we need be concerned with was the method and means, provided largely by applied physics, of acquisition and use. Supply, it was assumed, would automatically equal demand. The second assumption was that the boom was normal, so normal that most men did not realize its existence.

Turning to the period of the closing frontier, the last half century, we find ourselves standing face to face with our previous assumptions, beginning to see how utterly false they are. There will not always be a frontier, and there cannot be an everlasting boom derived from a source that is disappearing. True there is still an imbalance of population between the Metropolis of Europe and the Great Frontier countries, but immigration laws have cut off the current of adjustment. There is still an imbalance of wealth, the frontier countries having most of the raw materials; the currents of adjustment are still flowing from here to there, but so sluggishly that we have resorted to the force pump. The natural dynamics that operated effectively during the centuries of the open frontier have either been stopped artificially or made to flow artificially. Under these changed conditions, our boom-born institutions have run into crisis after crisis. Both democracy and capitalism have been in trouble since the first world war, and both have given ground for the first time in the modern era. There is now little excess room for the explosive increase in population and there is not enough food in the world for what we have. Who will say that the present situation would not be relieved if some Columbus would enter here and announce that he had brought us three or four rich and empty continents? Then we could be sure of a new lease on the life of the frontier boom, a new lease on the same kind of life we have been accustomed to lead. As it is we find ourselves dressed up in frontier clothes, fully equipped with a fine set of frontier ideas and institutions, and nowhere to go. We have now arrived near the end of an adventurous and exciting age, and our main problem is one of making adjustments to another age that is quite different in character.

Thus far I have said little about physics, though I have tried to picture the conditions surrounding its origin and accompanying its development. I have said that this booming world, full of movement and loaded with materials, was a physicist's paradise, but I also suggested that this paradise was abnormal, a pleasant purgatorial anteroom to a less abundant future state. It is not unthinkable that physics, like democracy and capitalism, may be given pause by the closing of the frontier and the end of the boom, that it too may bog down.

In the midst of the boom physics found unlimited opportunity to become practical, to apply its abstract principles to daily tasks. In its early stages it was concerned primarily with two elements, which I will make bold to call substance and energy. Its practical task was to apply the energy to the substance in such a manner as to procure or produce what would be useful to men. It performed this task so well that it set off a current in history that accelerated the revolution in human living more than anything else known. I refer to the industrial revolution, the first stages of which belonged almost exclusively to applied physics.

What I wish to call attention to is the close connection that existed between applied physics and the Great Frontier. I have said that applied physics deals with energy and substance. The energy used in the modern age has been mainly from the fossil fuels. The Great Frontier is rich in the fossil fuels, having about 56 percent of the world's coal and 54 percent of its petroleum. Europe has coal, but is almost destitute of petroleum. As for substance, stuff to be fabricated and moved, the United States probably has more than Western Europe. In short, the Great Frontier has supplied more than half the energy and a far greater proportion of the substance with which applied physics has worked its magic.

It was in the frontier, in the United States, that physics found the most favorable conditions for a practical demonstration of what it could do. Here men were few, laborers scarce, wages high, and resources abundant. Consequently there was a premium on any device that would convert the resources into wealth with a minimum of human labor. En-

51

ergy and substance being abundant and demand being great during this period, men could incur any expense that would create machines and provide the power to drive them. As a result the United States in the nineteenth century became an enormous laboratory of applied physics, and a further result of that was an accumulation of wealth equaled only by the destruction of resources.

During this happy period physics—or physicists—shared the false assumptions that both energy and substance were unlimited, that there was plenty more on the frontier, and that there would always be a frontier. Under present conditions applied physics faces the task of performing its services in a world of disappearing fossil energy and of declining substance.

Let us look at energy as represented by the fossil fuels. We may not know how much of it there is, but we do know that the total in storage is an absolute amount and that it cannot be increased by any art yet known to man. We also know that our use of fossil fuels is comparatively recent, and that its destruction is proceeding at an ever accelerating rate. Its total destruction, under the present process, is not only inevitable but in sight. Waldemar Kaempffert in *The New York Times* of September 20, 1953 wrote:

> Palmer Putnam of the Atomic Energy Commission turned up at Madison, Wisconsin, last week to tell the American Institute of Biological Sciences the now familiar story of the day when there is no more coal, no more oil, no more gas. What shall we do then for energy? . . . Putnam saw no salvation in atomic energy. . . . We have about three centuries to engage in research and experimenting . . . time enough to devise something that will work. There is no doubt that when the world stands face to face with no combustible fuel and no uranium or thorium, it will sink its differences in the common cause of keeping its factories going.

What the scientist is saying is that within three centuries the sources of energy on which our present civilization is based will be approaching depletion.

The case with the second element, the substance with which applied physics works, is not much different from that of energy. Many of the sources of our essential materials are being depleted in this rich country, and we are now importing some that we formerly exported. At the present rate of use in the face of increasing demands we should find ourselves bankrupt of our key materials at about the same time we are bankrupt of our accustomed form of energy. Looking back three hundred years, we see that physics played its role in the midst of increasing plenty; looking forward three hundred years, we see that it must in all probability play its role in increasing scarcity of both energy and substance.

From the vantage point of the present we see physics appear between the Metropolis of Europe and the Great Frontier, riding high on the boom when conditions were unusual and abnormal—and highly favorable to this science. Thus far it has been a prime creator of the wealth and luxury we enjoy. In reality physics has in all that time created nothing. It has moved things from one place to another and it has fabricated them, but it has not created any substance. On the contrary physics appears as the great destroyer of both energy and substance. In its first centuries—up to now— physics discounted the future for the present to help give us what Vernon L. Parrington called the Great Barbecue, paid for with irreplaceable capital.

In an imaginative exercise let us view physics in the role of fate. A master tragedian might represent it as a character with uncanny skill and evil intent concealed under the pleasing cloak of preliminary good works. Master of a magic formula for combining energy and substance, physics, like the Pied Piper, has lured men on to the luxury and extravagances of the Big Barbecue. But in doing this, it has progressively destroyed the very elements of its own magic. Seeing men turn on one another—as they have been doing since 1914— for what is left, physics, realizing that its own game is up and that its magic formula can no longer work, ends the play with its supreme gift for destruction, revealing its true character as a destroyer just when the curtain falls on the shattering ruin of civilization itself. By the law of the drama, the main character must see his predicament, he must struggle to avert disaster, but he is swept along to the inevitable end by forces he can not control, even though he may have originated them.

Since the tragedy has not yet occurred, except in token form, physics may yet have a choice as to what it is going to do in the time remaining. Historically it is faced with a decreasing supply of energy, a diminishing amount of substance, and the demands of an increasing number of people. It had great success in expanding the booming world of abnormal conditions. What will physics do now with a contracting world that is getting back to the normal prefrontier stage? It has known how to act on the false assumption of the infinite and unlimited. How will it respond to the unrelenting facts of the finite?

I have no doubt that the applied physicists will unfold many new devices, for they still have some time. I am sure that people will continue to say with wistful hopefulness that the physicists will open new frontiers and continue to work their old magic. They, along with their fellow scientists, will indeed be men of magic if they open anything comparable in magnitude or influence to what they, and all of us, had in the Great Frontier.

V GEOGRAPHICAL-HISTORICAL CONCEPTS
in AMERICAN HISTORY

J PROPOSE to discuss how a knowledge of geography and an interest in it has enabled me to understand history and make a good deal of sense out of some of it that I never otherwise would have been able to do. Some of you may be so devoted to objectivity, so determined to make a science out of what is so human and unscientific that you will not care to listen to a personal experience, written without footnotes. But since I have already lived more than my allotted time, spent more than half a century studying and teaching what I learned, I may be permitted to talk in a personal vein, on the assumption that if I am ever to speak intimately of what I have learned and how, I must do it soon.

Those who are acquainted with what I have written know that practically all the history I have done, and certainly the best of it, is based solidly and consciously on geography, on the character of the land where the action described took place. And had I not done this I probably would not be on this program tonight.

The task of preparing this paper caused me to try to recall the origin of my interest in geography. Probably it dates back to my boyhood when I roamed the surrounding pastures with my dog and unconsciously absorbed some knowledge of the land forms, noted that the grass grew in the valleys and the rocks on the high hills. My real awakening, however, came when I began teaching a country school, and found that one of the courses I had to teach was called physical geography. There was a red clothbound text, entitled *Physical Geography* by a man named W. E. Davis. I had never seen the book or heard of the subject before, and so it became necessary for me to read it pretty closely in order to stay ahead of the class. This book differed from Wentworth's arithmetic and Reed and Kellog's grammar in that it dealt with things I knew about. It differed from political geography where I had to memorize all the states in the union and their capitals, memorize the names of five oceans which I knew only by reputation, and learn that Belize was the capital of British Honduras. It differed from spelling because I did not have to do puzzles with letters, getting them in exact order to form a word which often was pronounced as if spelled in another way. But here in Davis's *Physical Geography* was something that made sense from the first, something I had seen when hunting horses in the early morning. From the book I went back to the pasture, and sure enough there things were going on just like the author said they should. It was a wonderful experience, and I have never gotten over it. I have always regretted that physical geography fell a victim to progressive education and was removed from the curriculum.

In my third year in the University I took a course called Institutional History, given by Lindley Miller Keasbey. This was the second and most important step in providing me a geographic base from which to view human activity. Keasbey had studied in Germany, knew Frederich Ratzel and J. J. E.

56

Reclus, Ellsworth Huntington and the rest, and made us read at their books. What I got from Keasbey, in addition to a method of thinking, was the relation between environment and civilization, and a curiosity to learn more about it. Different people have different keys to the half hidden secrets of a subject. Here was my key, this relation of culture and environment, the connection between what men did and the conditions surrounding them, conditions which in some measure prescribe their action and dictate the results. Not for a moment would I claim that this is the only key, but it is as good as any other, better than some, and the best for me.

Modern geology, for which physical geography is the craftsman and artisan, was founded by the man who first perceived that the physical forces that formed the layers of the earth are the same forces operating today on the surface. Erosion and sedimentation go on now just as they did in a similar climate one million or ten million years ago. The man who discovered this elementary fact was James Button, an Englishman, who published his *Theory of the Earth* in 1795. He was a forerunner of Lyell and Darwin, for the theory of the earth's slow evolution was implicit in the simple principle he enunciated, seventy-five years before Darwin and Wallace announced the more famous one.

The consoling thing about physical geography is that it is firm under your feet. It provides a fairly permanent base on which to lay down a foundation and erect a superstructure with poetry, literature and religion. If you would understand many features of the American West, and especially the more arid portions, read the Old Testament.

The critics dearly love to sink their teeth in those of us who elect to approach history, civilization, if you please, through geography, by way of the physical environment. Critics charge that such an approach results in rank materialism, and if they are crowded a little they will mention Karl Marx, and link your name with his. Of course I do not know why they react in this manner, but I suspect it is due to frustration. They may resent the orderly manner in which the story of a culture unfolds, once it is based solidly on the ground. The logic seems to make them mad.

In defense of the method I may point out that it coincides in a general way with the evolution of the culture which we are seeking to understand. The whole action occurred on some piece of land, and is related in numerous ways to the land and the climate. Whatever is produced, whether baskets or pottery, whether corn or wheat, or palaces or hovels, or poetry or painting, is related to the land and that relationship can be discovered. The land is the matrix out of which the culture grows.

What I have said by way of introduction is intended to explain my bent towards geography and the philosophy that has sustained me while I stuck to my chosen point of view. For the remainder of the paper, I shall cite some specific examples of geographic-historic concepts I have developed and found personally rewarding, both as a student and as a teacher. In presenting these concepts around which I have written books and articles, it will be necessary for me to make reference to my own work. I trust you will pardon my assumption that you do not know these books in detail, but I have found the assumption safe enough with other audiences.

My first, and probably best known, book is *The Great Plains*, published in 1931. Since I was to become a geographic historian, I could not have been more fortunate in selecting a subject for the beginning. Fortunate because, as all of you know, the Great Plains of the American West is a land where the physical forces are almost overwhelming, so imperious that no man and no institution has been able to ignore them, and all have had to adapt to them. In another respect I was fortunate in that I could start with a clean land. The very forces that man had to overcome had been so strong as to keep the land naked almost to the years of my earliest memory. The whole evolution of permanent civilization there, if we except the Indians and a fringe of Spaniards, took place only yesterday. Here was a situation made to order for one who wanted to examine the relationship between a human culture and a physical environment. There was still another feature that made the task seem fairly easy, after it was done. The American people who were to take the Plains came from an entirely different kind of land. These Americans had had no previous experience with a land so treeless, so level, so arid. They came to it in almost complete ignorance of it, and they had to invent, adapt and devise quickly or perish. The break with their past was clean, clear and sharp, and the trail they left was recent and plain to follow. I had the benefit of the marvelous contrast between the Western Plains and the Eastern Woodland. The contrast was much sharper for the Americans than for the Spaniards who came from an arid land and knew better than the Americans how to deal with it. Another thing in my favor, which I discovered as I went along, was that the Great Plains region is a fairly distinct geographic unit. It is almost as good as an island, better than the hydrographic basin. By sheer luck I had hit upon the easiest region in the entire country in which to study the relations between people and the land they occupied. For me it was an intellectual windfall of gigantic proportions and no one knows this better than I.

In the process of telling the story that unfolded I was compelled to get an education, and I had to do it on my own. Since the story was to be that of environment and civilization I had to learn about both. Since the whole concept was based on the land I had to learn geology, how the Great Plains were built and graded by the swinging rivers which came out of the west spewing sand and soil to form a great debris apron spread at the Eastern foot of the Rocky Mountains. Then there were the High Plains, standing above grade, like a table set down on a level floor of a greater plain. I had to learn why this table stood up there in such curious fashion, so that you have to go up hill to it whether you approach it from the east or from the west. I learned from Willard D. Johnson that it is a survival, etched away on the east by water erosion, on the west in grotesque fashion by what I have called arid-land erosion, and what is left was preserved by a solid turf of short grass.

Upon this base I laid down the flora and fauna, all bearing the mark of the environment, and this meant excursions into botany and zoology. Then I invaded anthropology, and introduced the Plains Indians who were as beautifully adapted to the land as the mesquite grass or the jackrabbits and antelope. You see, I was building from the ground up, laying one block form upon another, pretty sure by this time what I would come out with, for there was remarkable harmony all along the way.

Then, in 1528 and 1540, came the disharmony in the guise of the Europeans. The Spaniards, who, as I have said, knew arid lands, might have made a success of it had they thought it really worthwhile. With Mexico City as a center they probed northward, using a pioneering machine which they had found to be very successful. This machine consisted of three agents, the conqueror to subdue, the convertor to save, and the entrepreneur to exploit and make a profit, the conquistador, the missionary, and the encomendero. Selecting a vantage point at the southern end of the Great Plains I watched them come. When they hit the arid country the economic agent failed for there was no profit, and the encomienda system was abolished in 1720. Then they came on with the missionaries and soldiers until they struck the Plains tribes, Comanches and Apaches. These they could never convert, and they abolished the mission system in 1812. This left only the soldiers who were by now no match for the mounted Comanches and Apaches. The whole Spanish advance northward had been stopped long before Napoleon picked Europe up in his teeth and shook it loose from its monarchs and empires. Knowing the Plains as a land of recoil, the whole Spanish story made sense.

60

Having disposed of the Spaniards, I moved over from the Southern end of the Plains corridor to its eastern edge where I could observe another breed of men tackle the job at which the Spaniards had failed. And I might here call your attention to what I have called the vantage point. My vantage point differs, I think, from that of most American historians. They move with the actors into the land, meeting events and obstacles as they present themselves. My method, and it has been used in both *The Great Plains* and *The Great Frontier*, is to take a vantage point on the land, and watch the actors approach it, knowing in advance what they will meet up with, and having at least some idea of how they will react to it.

My vantage point for observing the American approach to the Great Plains was on the dividing line between the woodland and the plain, between the prairie and the forest, where the trees left off and the grass began, and it was again from the south end, approximately on the 98th meridian.

With the opening of the second quarter of the 19th century, these Americans, moving on a ragged front, came out of the woods with the axe, the long rifle, and the boat, things they had found so serviceable for more than two centuries. They came without a government sponsored system of pioneering, such as the Spaniards had, but each man was for himself, and each was free to try whatever system he wanted. This coming out of the woods was the most momentous experience the pioneers had had since the initial one when they landed on the Atlantic shore. In describing the migration of his own family, and their emergence from the forest, Herbert Quick said, "It was the end of Book I of our history."

It was a most exciting experience I had as a historian just to stand there on the 98th meridian in Texas, look north to Canada, with a wall of timber and much water on the right hand and a sea of grass and practically no water on the left hand, and watch the antics of these people as they crept like insects out of the familiar country into one that was mysterious and strange. The story broke up here into a series of topics, each topic concerned with some adaptation they were compelled to make.

They had fought Indians all the way west, but never such Indians as they met on the Plains. These were the first mounted Indians the Americans had ever fought and by far the most nomadic. The Americans, really the Texans, had to mount horses to deal with them, but when they did they found their weapons were wholly unsuited to mounted combat. The Texans organized a mobile, mounted force, the Texas Rangers, the oldest organization of its kind in the world, and the first institutional adaptation to the Plains environment. The Texas Rangers then discovered the imperfect Colt revolver, which had been rejected elsewhere, told Colt how to perfect it for a mounted man. The revolver was the first mechanical or technological adaptation to the Plains.

Thus armed and mounted, the Texan learned to handle cattle on horseback, the Spanish longhorns that ran wild in the semi-desert south of San Antonio. After the Civil War, these Texans gathered the herds which had now spread north, drove them up the trails to establish the Cattle Kingdom in the seventeen western states, thus bringing the first permanent occupants to the Great Plains.

In the meantime the humbler people were nibbling at the eastern edge. Though they had perfected the American axe, they had little use for it here because there were practically no trees. The boat had served them well, but now there was no use for the boat because there were no lakes and no streams. The log cabin, the standard pioneer home, never, as Powell said, crossed the plains. For the same reason there were no rails, and in most places rocks formed the only fences they had known. This fence problem was not solved until 1873 when three farmers on the prairie in Illinois invented barbed wire. The six-inch bored well put an end to the "Old Oaken Bucket" which would have fallen to staves before it gathered any moss. The windmill was adapted and became the symbol of habitation. The law pertaining to land was badly bent and that pertaining to water was modified in all the seventeen states, and completely abrogated in eight of them. When the English common law is abrogated by Anglo-Americans there has to be a reason greater than the whim of a judge, jury or legislator. The eastern dirt-pushing plows would not turn the western sod, and the nameless blacksmiths lengthened the point until it cut like a knife; they changed the slope of the wing so that it would turn the heavy soil with its surface of turf upside down. The principles of dry farming were discovered in California or Utah, and the Department of Agriculture ransacked the deserts of the world to find drought resistant crops.

And this panorama of history, filled with some heroism, much tragedy, pathos and that grim humor which men make of their hardships, is what I saw as I watched these people tackle the western half of this country, the nature of which I already knew. Knowing the land as I did in 1931 I could have told them what to expect when they made the venture, but of course such is the nature of human beings that they would not have listened. The way they learned for themselves is their history. The way they told about it in song, poetry and story is their literature, the reflection of their experience in the mirror of memory.

And so I ended *The Great Plains* with a look at the literature which may come as a surprise to those who wonder if the Great Plains has produced any. Starting with the most substantial feature, the land, I wound up with the most etherial, and from the geology at the bottom to the literature which crowned the superstructure everything was tied together with a harmony that was not forced. And perhaps that harmony is what makes those who do not find any mad.

When I finished I thought I had said all I had to say about the American West. But I must now call your attention to the fact that the story was incomplete. You will recall that I had stood mentally at a selected vantage point and watched the people, both the Spaniards and the Americans, come into the strange land. I had dealt with the people *in motion* and observed them as they struggled with their basic problems. But now, by 1900–1950, they had settled down, fastened themselves to the soil, built their cities, arranged themselves in some sort of pattern on the land they had taken. A moving society had become a stationary one, a ground-based civilization. I had not examined the pattern they formed, and did not do so for twenty-five years.

About 1955 I decided to go out and look at the country again. That summer I drove from Texas to California with a friend who had some business in Las Vegas. I hardly knew what I was looking for, but as always I was fascinated by the weird land forms, the distances, the deserts. The next summer I went alone, north to the Canadian border in Montana. By this time I had found my question, and when you find your question, if it is the right one, you are half way home. My question was this: What makes this country what it is? What keeps it that way, almost unchanged, in spite of man's puny efforts? What gives the West its special character?

From Montana I turned south, keeping to those states just east of the Pacific tier, barely touching eastern California. I traveled in the desert all the way, spacing my journey so that I could sleep in the high mountains where it was cool. I did not hurry, but put in for a week or two at Salt Lake City, Reno, Las Vegas, and other less interesting places. Here I sought out the book stores, bought the local books, read them in the hotel, and then went out to see for myself what the authors were talking about. What keeps the West the way it is? I asked myself, as I looked out across a vast expanse of greasewood hemmed in by mountains fifty miles apart, with no living thing visible? What keeps the West the way it is, I asked. Then in the center of the vast place I found a river which I followed until it disappeared for lack of water. In Utah I stood on the shore of a strange inland sea, the Great Salt Lake, and asked the same question. Looking to the horizon I could make out the old shore of Lake Bonneville which has now shrunk to a briny fragment. In Nevada I saw hardby the Boulder Dam, and elsewhere, a limitless land, almost devoid of vegetation, smoking under the August sun as if it were just pulled from the fire yesterday. Variations of these same scenes I saw in Arizona and New Mexico, but as I turned east, after interminable miles, I found the land leveling out and the vegetation changing, and finally I was on the plains of which I had made so much. I saw the plains now as I had never seen them before.

Surely, I said to myself, I have seen a land 2000 miles long and several hundred miles wide where there has been a great fire. This fire is not yet quite out for the land in many parts is still smoking. It has burned up the substance, and is still so hot that but few people can get close to it. They have backed off from it, into California and Oregon, into Texas and Oklahoma and Kansas, forming a circle close enough to feel the heat, and to occasionally be scorched by it. Whatever made them back off is what gives the West its special character.

Then I began to recall what I had read but not noticed because I had not yet asked the right question. Coronado, Moscoso, Lewis and Clark, Pike, Greeley, Marcy, Jefferson Davis and Daniel Webster, had all talked of a desert. Long made a map of it—The Great American Desert he called it—and it got into the geographies and histories, but the chambers of commerce abolished it. From what I had seen I decided that the desert did not know that it had been abolished. There it was, as hot as ever, making the people stand back. I now had the answer to my question. It is the desert that makes the West what it is and keeps it that way. Again I had found the answer to my question in geography.

This concept of the desert gave me a new vantage point. This time I would take my stand in the heart of the desert to survey the society whose coming there I had examined with so much care. These people were no longer in motion. They had discovered by now what they could and could not do, and they had formed a pattern which could be described because it is relatively permanent. I was now ready to return to the books to see if the facts supported the thesis. The most dependable source, for the economics, was the Statistical Abstract. I cannot go into detail but I can describe the pattern of wealth in relation to the desert. I have already alluded to the fact that the people have formed a great circle around the margins of the desert. The wealth has done the same thing, whether you measure bank deposits, tractors, or cattle. The only exception I found is the sheep population. This means that economically the West, because of the desert, is a land of deficiencies. It forms a great depression, if represented on a graph. Such people as are found in the desert states are clustered around the scanty supply of water, and even this scanty population is pressing hard on the water supply. This means that today we have in the American West an oasis civilization. Even around the margins where great cities have grown up, there is a desperate water problem in San Antonio, Dallas, Fort Worth, Oklahoma City on the eastern margin, and Los Angeles.

Now let us look at the pattern as formed by the seventeen western states. The heart of the desert—if I may use the worn out term—comprises the eight so-called mountain states, New Mexico, Arizona, Colorado, Wyoming, Nevada, Idaho, Utah, and Montana. These I have called the desert states. The six states to the east, Texas, Oklahoma, Kansas, Nebraska, and the two Dakotas are then the Eastern Desert Rim states, all of them semi-arid to arid in their western portions. They form the right flank of the desert and constitute the major portion of the plains area. To the west of the desert states are Washington, Oregon, and California. They form the western desert rim, and all are arid in their eastern sections. They are the left flank of the desert. So, on this map, you see the seventeen western states as they line up with reference to the concept of the controlling desert. I wish to call your attention to the simplicity of this map. You will note that the states stand in tiers, with a north-south axis. That is the way the West is laid out in nature, on a north-south axis. Each tier has a dominant characteristic. The eastern tier is primarily a plains tier, the central is mountain, and the western is a sea slope. But the common feature that spreads over them all is a blanket of aridity, shading off to humid on the margins.

The logic of this arrangement leads me to suggest that the Census Bureau may well take a new look at the divisions it now uses in its regional map of the United States. The trouble seems to have arisen when the census divisions were established, making the Mississippi River a dividing line. The Mississippi does not, in my opinion, divide up the adjacent states on its opposite banks; it unites them so far as culture is concerned. The Mississippi does not mark the generally accepted division between the East and the West. The dividing line between these two great regions runs along the western boundary of the first tier of states beyond the river. The West begins in this second tier, what I have called the Eastern Desert Rim states, and this fact is recognized in official maps of the West. The Census Bureau does not, however, recognize this fact in its regional divisions. It puts Louisiana and Arkansas in the West South Central division; it puts Missouri, Iowa and Minnesota in the West North Central. Then it sets up to the East the East North Central and the East South Central. I doubt there is anyone in my hearing who has not worked with the census divisions who can keep these four regions in mind or name the states that comprise each one.

Here then is my suggestion for possible consideration of the Census Bureau.

1. Move the line dividing the East and the West from the Mississippi over to the western boundaries of the first tier of states, beyond the Mississippi. This will make the map of the regions conform to the two grand divisions, the East and the West.

2. Move Arkansas and Louisiana over with Mississippi and Tennessee to form the South Central region of only six states.

3. Move Missouri, Iowa and Minnesota over with Illinois and Wisconsin to form a middle western block of eight states, the North Central region.

By making these changes we would get rid of two categories that are quite confusing, and have no more than eight states in any region. The three divisions in the West would all be true western states, and could be called the Plains region, the Mountain region, and the Pacific region. This is logical, simple, and in conformity with both geography and history. The Census divisions would then appear as on this revamped map.

When I received this assignment, I had in mind using *The Great Frontier*, published in 1953, to further illustrate how much intelligible history can be drawn from studying the relationship between the environment and the civilization. Here I used a much bigger canvas. The territory, consisting of all the new lands discovered by Columbus and his associates, which I called the Great Frontier, lacks the unity of the Great Plains, and is a unit only in that it was all wilderness when tackled by the Europeans from the Metropolis. But again I selected a vantage point *in the frontier*, observed the people from the Metropolis as they invaded it, noted their reaction as they adapted their institutions to it. Most historians have marched with the invaders, emphasizing what they did to the wilderness; I stood in the wilderness and tried to observe what it did to the invaders. Time does not permit me to develop this exciting experience further.

By way of conclusion, I want to repeat. I was extremely fortunate in my first effort in selecting an area beautifully adapted to a study of the relationship between geography and human action. When I finished *The Great Plains*, I tried to do a parallel study of the Eastern Woodland, but found it impossible for me. The land was too complex, and

68

the evolution of the society was too hard to follow. I had to leave it to the geographers.

As I see it now, *The Great Plains* as it appeared in 1931 was incomplete. It was, and is, incomplete because it was confined to telling the dynamic story of the movement of the people into the land. Actually it did not cover the entire West, but only the level portions of it.

I regret to say it took me twenty-five years to take the next step, and to find in the geography the key to the entire West of which the plains region is only a part. This key I finally found in the concept of the great desert, with the plains on its right flank and the Pacific coast on its left flank. When I discovered this, I saw that in *The Great Plains* I had in reality dressed down the right flank of the desert. Taking the desert as the center I now understand not only the struggle the people had in going out there, but also why they have formed the present patterns there. At last I think I know what makes the West, what it is and what keeps it that way.

Finally, I may point out, before someone else does, that the historian who lays his foundation on the ground and builds his historical superstructure on it, is likely to come out with an assurance that can be annoying. This is especially true when he deals with a desert, which dictates so imperiously to man. He keeps looking at the desert, glowing and palpitating in the sun, making men stand back, reversing the normal relative value of land and water, frustrating man's most determined efforts, making him bend to its will. There is a terrible logic about it, and the historian begins to follow this logic. It leads him into strange places, and the first thing he knows he is making suggestions to the geographers, map makers and to the Census Bureau as if he were their equal.

VI A TEXAS MUSEUM
of NATURAL HISTORY in HOUSTON

Natural History. Formerly, the study, description, and classification of animals, plants, minerals, and other natural objects, thus including the modern sciences of zoology, botany, mineralogy, etc., in so far as they existed at that time. Now commonly restricted to a study of these subjects in a more or less unsystematic way.

Webster, Unabridged.

T HE ABOVE definition of natural history gives us a starting point for considering a Texas Museum of Natural History located in the city of Houston. It sets the limits within which any museum of natural history ought to begin its work. It makes obvious that the scientists of one sort or another will play the leading role in providing the materials, the displays and the dioramas which will entertain and instruct the public and furnish source material for students and scholars who desire to pursue intensive investigations in the various fields represented. The duty of the personnel, from the director to the technicians, will be to exhibit the materials in such a way as to make them attractive to the general public and informative to the student and scholar. And these people, too, must have scientific training.

It would seem from the above definition, and analysis, that the historian has little place in a museum of natural history, and I suspect an examination would reveal that professional historians do not play any prominent part in professional museums, once they are built and launched on their programs. As a historian I must disclaim any particular knowledge of the finer points of museums. I do not know how to build one, equip one, or run it, and I certainly do not know how to raise money for one.

What I do know something about is the environment which surrounds Houston, and which a museum built here should reflect in miniature and which it will have an opportunity to serve. If this museum does not reflect the environment around it then it will not be a good museum. It will not be honest because it is false to the region. It could easily become a morgue, a place for stuffed owls and such other items as influential donors may wish to get out of their attics and cellars. I have seen such so-called museums and found them very depressing.

In what I just said I used the singular, environment. Perhaps I may be permitted to substitute the plural, environments, as I wish to show the relation of a Texas Museum of Natural History in Houston to four distinct regions or environments, or four geographic features which comprise the environment of Texas, and extend far beyond Texas in four directions. If a museum can be made to represent these four regions which meet, contend with and complement one another in Texas, then it will also represent much greater regions *beyond* Texas, and similar regions in all parts of the world. In short, such a museum would be local, state wide, national, and universal.

71

You will note that I have used the term, a Texas Museum of Natural History *in Houston*. I doubt very much that a Houston Museum of Natural History would be worth building, scarcely worth seeing by anyone but antiquarians. It would appeal to few students and to fewer scholars. It would not be worthy of what this city aspires to be, and gives considerable promise of becoming. What I am talking about is a museum *in Houston* which would remove all reason any other metropolis in this state might have for building a Texas Museum of Natural History.

Therefore let us forget Houston for the moment and talk about Texas. I spoke a moment ago of the four environments that meet in the state. I now call your attention to the fact that they meet in Texas, but that, big as Texas is, it contains only a small part of each of these great natural features. I also want to say that Texas is the only state in the union where all four of these features are found. What is more, they do not exist together in any other area the size of Texas anywhere else on this continent. Their combination and juxtaposition here are unique.

The four features to which I refer are as follows:

The Great Eastern Woodland
The Great Western Plains
The Southwestern Desert
The Southeastern Sea

On this map of Texas I have indicated these four features and the part of Texas where they are found. The Eastern Woodland is green, the Great Plains is gray, the Desert is pink, and the Sea is of course blue. Houston stands by the sea, on the western edge of the Great Forest, where we see the first pines, on the eastern edge of the Great Plains, and fortunately for Houston, some two hours' drive from the Desert. Houston receives its tribute from all four, and is what it is because all four pay that tribute. Take one of them away and Houston would be altered; take all of them away and it would be nothing.

On the second map I have shown that each of these regions, the Woodland of East Texas, the Plains of the Panhandle, the Desert of the Trans Pecos, the Big Bend and the whole Rio Grande from Brownsville to El Paso, and the Mexican Gulf,—each is but a small fragment of a greater woodland extending to the Atlantic, of a greater Plain extending to Canada, of a greater Desert extending to Utah and California and including all northern Mexico, and of a greater Sea which wraps itself around the continents of the world. By being true to the local, we approach the universal.

A line drawn from Brownsville due north, approximating the 98th meridian, separates the humid and forested American East from the American West, with its plains and deserts. This line separates two botanical and zoological kingdoms which meet in Texas. Plant life and animal life on the two sides of this line are quite different, and these differences are found in Texas. All bird watchers and ornithologists know that Texas exhibits more species and varieties of bird life than any comparable areas. It is the flyway for the migrating birds from the great eastern woodland and the great western plains. It is a sort of funnel through which they pass on their seasonal flights to and from the tropical seas and the tropical lands of South America. This explains why Texas is the bird watcher's paradise.

Let us leave now the world of nature and introduce a little history to illustrate what has happened in human affairs, our own affairs, as a result of the meeting of these environmental features. People wonder why there is so much of the spectacular about this state, something so dramatic in its history. The spectacular and dramatic character of Texas history is not hard to understand if we look at the state in terms of these four natural features.

For the moment we will leave the sea, the 350 miles of Gulf Coast, aside and consider the three land features indicated on this map. The forest, the plain and the desert not only meet in Texas, but they seem to contend with one another for supremacy. Even the climates contend, the hot winds from the desert, the cold blasts from the plains, and the soft south winds from the Gulf make the weather variable and almost unpredictable. While the snow blankets the Panhandle, people pick tropical fruits in the Rio Grande Valley. While the people of East Texas often have too much water, those of West Texas rarely have enough.

Each of the three land regions has produced its own culture, and almost its own civilization, a woodland culture in East Texas, a plains culture in the Panhandle, and a desert culture along the upper Rio Grande and in the Trans-Pecos. The tempestuous history of Texas from 1820 to 1845 reflects the struggle for supremacy in Texas among three cultures. From the Eastern Woodland came the Americans under Stephen F. Austin and Sam Houston; on the grasslands to the northwest stood the Comanches on horseback who contested every step made in that direction; from the southwest came the desert culture of Mexico which fought as best it could to hold its more powerful enemy back. The Texas Revolution marked the culmination of this struggle, and the miniature battle fought on the San Jacinto plain some twenty miles from here settled the issue. The existence of the independent Republic for nine years was but a brief pause as Texas moved *politically* from the domination of the Plains Indians and the desert Mexicans to domination by the men from the Eastern Woodland.

Though this revolution and move settled the political issue, they did not decide the cultural struggle. When the Americans—now Texans—moved into the plains and into the desert they came face to face with environments which refused to yield much to them. They had to adapt themselves to the land. Two examples, one for the plain and one for the desert, will illustrate the point.

All previous attempts by the Anglo-Americans to occupy the Great Plains had all but failed. Then the Texans found

74

the longhorns, wild Spanish cattle, south of San Antonio. They found the Spanish horses running wild on the prairie. They borrowed the Spanish-Mexican gear, saddle, bit, and lariat, they caught the mustangs and learned to handle cattle on horseback, the first Americans to do this. There, where men learned to handle cattle on horseback, the American cowboy was born, and it was he, the Texan, who followed the cattle north and west over the sea of grass and founded the cattle kingdom in the seventeen western states. These cowboys and cattlemen were the first permanent white occupants of the plains.

The second example is found in the southwestern desert. It has to do with two new methods of farming, irrigation farming where there was water, and dry-land farming where there was not enough for irrigation. There are numerous other examples of these adaptations, but for the present these must suffice.

It is clear that when these Texans from the Eastern Woodland adapted themselves to the new conditions they encountered on the plains and on the desert, they began to vary from what they and their ancestors had been. This variation reflects the varied conditions they found within their own state. It goes far to explain why there are so many kinds of Texans.

Again let me illustrate with specific examples. In any city or in any club you can find from East Texas the southern cotton planter and the lumberman and loggers; you can find the cowboy and cattleman from the plain, mixed with the dry-land wheat and maize growers; you can find the wool and mohair grower, and the irrigation farmer who produces citrus fruit in the subtropical Rio Grande valley and long staple cotton at El Paso. The mark of the region is on the men from the region, and about all they have in common is that they are all Texans, and sometimes too boastful of it.

The reason the Texan never meets a stranger is because nearly all strangers are native to this land. The Texan moves within his own state through almost the whole gamut of American experience. He is separated for fifteen hundred miles from a foreign nation speaking a different language, and having a different culture. He can holler to these foreign neighbors across a narrow and ofttimes dry stream. There is no other such border of equal length in the nation. The Texan can fish in salt water for 350 miles along the Gulf Coast, and if he is inclined to leave the state, he can step on a ship from the Texas shore and remain in Texas water for nine miles out. The only experience he can have in the United States but cannot have in Texas is riding on a subway and skiing. All other experiences of the woodland, the plain, the desert and the sea can be had in some part of the state. If the individual Texan is not cosmopolitan, he should be, for his is in a cultural sense the most cosmopolitan state in the union.

I wish to return for a moment to Webster's definition of Natural History. "Formerly, the study, description, and classification of animals, plants, minerals, and other natural objects, thus including the modern sciences of zoology, botany, mineralogy, etc., insofar as they existed at that time." You will note that Natural History was originally concerned with natural objects, before those objects became the subjects of the formalized sciences we know today. Natural History goes back to the time when men collected natural objects which interested them, but which they did not yet understand. The first two meanings of the term as given by the New Oxford Dictionary are as follows:

1. "A work dealing with the properties of natural objects; a scientific account of any object written along these lines."

2. "The aggregate of facts relating to natural objects."

I mention this early and original meaning to emphasize again that Natural History is concerned primarily with sciences, with what was on the ground before science began to tinker with it and transform it. It does not follow that a modern Museum of Natural History would stop with an exhibition of natural objects before science was applied to them, before this tinkering and transforming took place. While science is concerned with natural objects, it has never created one. It has never made a tree, a drop of oil, an ounce of sulphur, or a pound of coal. As powerful as science is, it has until now left creation to the Creator. It has, however, done marvelous things, some of them quite terrifying, with what it found—with natural objects.

A modern Museum of Natural History would therefore, in my opinion, be greatly concerned with what science has done with these natural objects. Let me illustrate with two or three examples, taken from the Texas scene. A Museum of Natural History would show, either in diorama or on the ground, an East Texas forest, and that natural forest exhibit would be followed by exhibits of all the commodities made from the forest. There would be an exhibit of how oil and gas were created and are trapped in the earth, followed by exhibits of how it has been extracted from the time Drake sank his little well in Pennsylvania to the present offshore drilling. Sulphur also exists far below the surface, either in pure form or in sour gas. In pure form it is extracted by driving steam into the sulphur bed, steam of such heat as to melt the sulphur and with such force as to raise it to the surface in molten form where it is solidified into the yellow mountains we see at the Texas mines. This whole process could well be shown in miniature, together with the various uses of sulphur, uses which range from curing the itch to manufacturing linoleum and hundreds of other articles. A proper Museum of Natural History could reveal in visual form the mysteries of the universe and simplify to some extent the complexities of the industries which have made Texas rich and Houston a booming metropolis.

My function here, I suppose, is to stir your imagination as to the possibilities of a great museum, stir it so much as to loosen, or enable you to loosen, somebody's purse strings. This museum, as I visualize it, is going to cost somebody some money, a great deal more money than a mere college professor can imagine, even a college professor with considerable imagination. This imagination and a knowledge of the land, plus an understanding of the land's influence on human culture, are all I have to offer. But if you will build a museum worthy of the opportunity you have, you will indeed jar the imagination of the cultural and intellectual world, and you will have on your hands a considerable traffic problem because there will be nothing comparable to it elsewhere in the country.

Since I have departed so far from my field of conventional history as to talk about science and a museum to exhibit it, I might as well go further and speak of a building to house it. Here I am invading, tentatively and with misgivings, the realms of architecture, my knowledge of which equals but does not surpass my knowledge of museums. The architects will, I trust, bear in mind that I speak as a historian who sees architecture in relation to the land that produces and supports it. When such a new enterprise as this is being contemplated, it is customary to send committees on tour, with all expenses paid, to see what has been done elsewhere, and that is a proper procedure. But this should not be a borrowing tour; it should be an educational one.

I am well acquainted with a great institution that borrowed its architecture from a cold northern climate and set it down in a sun-washed and semi-tropical land. In both the museum and the library—and especially in the museum— the architects put as much glass as possible on the west side so as to catch the direct rays of the afternoon sun, and at the same time they cut off as much breeze as they could from the south and east. For five months out of the year these buildings would hatch eggs if somebody would turn them over once a day. Now that institution is spending a million dollars on air-conditioning to make habitable buildings which they spent five million dollars to make intolerable. Here in Texas, where there is room to spare, they erected a twenty-four story tower and put a Greek temple on top because a member of the building committee taught Greek and wanted an office there. He is gone now but the damned Greek temple is still up there, two hundred feet higher than any Greek ever was. The library was constructed in such a manner that hardly a book is visible, and with such complexity that you have to go upstairs in order to get downstairs, and when you get down there you are likely to have to inquire the way out. You may think I am exaggerating, but I am actually dealing in understatement. So much for borrowed architecture.

I shall not be so bold as to make suggestions to those architects who will have the grand opportunity of designing a Museum of Natural History in Houston. Their opportunity, however, is overmatched by their responsibility. Their opportunity is *now*, and it is transient; their responsibility extends into the future, as long as what they design and build lasts. Though it would not be proper for me to make positive suggestions, I may be permitted to pose two questions.

1. Would it be architecturally feasible to design a museum building in the shape of the map of Texas? In such a museum the displays could be put in that portion of the building which represents the same part of Texas. A tour of the museum would be a miniature tour of the state and of the larger regions that extend so far beyond it. The forest products, for example, would be in the east as would the iron and steel. The great windows of the southeast would look out on a miniature Gulf of Mexico, with the more important sand dune islands such as Padre and Mustang showing above the water. I understand that machines have been devised that could send miniature breakers in on the miniature shelfing beach just as we see at Galveston or

on Padre. Next to this would be the marine display. The landscaping around the building would conform to the Texas scene, pines on the east, grass to the north, and the barren desert with its ocatillio, Joshua trees, greasewood and sage to the southwest. It can all be done in Houston, though there might be some trouble here with the desert flora.

2. But if the architects tell us that a building shaped like the map of Texas is wholly impractical, then let us consider a more radical departure, an entirely new kind of museum. Could they design a replica of Texas, not in the building itself, but on the ground? That is my second question. Then we would have on the ground not only the natural vegetation, but also the topography of the state, including the major rivers. From sea level on the Gulf coast we would ascend by steps leading up to the shore of the ancient sea as seen at Columbus, then to the Balcones Fault at Austin, through the Hill Country, and on to the Caprock of the High Plains and the towering peaks of the Guadalupe Mountains near El Paso and the ghost-like Chisos of the Big Bend.

The dioramas could be set at appropriate places on the map where they belonged, or in small scattered buildings designed to be inconspicuous in the landscape. This in effect would be an open air museum, a museum in the round, as different from the conventional one as a tourist court differs from a grand hotel. Of course there would have to be a main building for administration and for scholarly work, but the attraction for the throngs would be in an outdoor tour of Texas as it once was.

I am aware that both these suggestions are quite unconventional, and my feelings will not be hurt at all if they are rejected as impractical or absurd. I would like to point out, however, that Frank Lloyd Wright came to be recognized as a genius by breaking the architectural conventions. He built out of the earth rather than borrowing something and clapping it down on it, like the Greek temple and the Italian villa. Through him and others somewhat less daring, creative architecture has moved from Europe to America. On November 6, 1959, *The Times Literary Supplement* of London devoted almost the entire issue to "The American Imagination." It carried a review of Ian McCallum's *Architecture U.S.A.* and Frank Lloyd Wright's *A Testament*. The reviewer stated that as of today the United States is the most vital architectural region in the world, vital because its architects are doing bold, unconventional and appropriate things. The reviewer thinks that in the future the new grand tour for architects will be from Europe to America rather than the other way, as in the past. It is not beyond the realm of the reasonable that the Texas Museum of Natural History could be something that that future grand tour of architects would not want to miss.

Houston is in a fortunate position to do just this, but the decision must be made now. One advantage is that the work can start on clean and uncluttered ground. "There are," says *The Times* review, "three conditions for great architecture." These are "a lively building industry, creative freedom and conspicuous expenditure, and all three exist in the United States and nowhere else." The daily building permits in the Houston papers run into the millions, a lively building industry. Architecturally Houston offers creative freedom, and it is notable for conspicuous expenditure. It fulfills all the conditions as few other cities in the nation do.

Houston has another qualification not mentioned by the English reviewer. It is already a center of learning. It supports a symphony orchestra and it maintains a fine arts museum. It has three universities, one supported by a church, one by an adequate endowment, and the youngest one—and by far the largest—by courage, promise, and a sense of destiny. The scholars in these universities will contribute much to such an institution as we visualize, and receive much from it. There are other colleges within the city, parochial and private, which will benefit and be benefited. Houston is surrounded by smaller cities which have junior colleges with eager students and active faculties. As for the public school students, they will simply cover the place up, and they will come by buses and by car to see such a museum; they will come from all over the state, and from far beyond.

In view of all these circumstances, I wish to express a final opinion. It is that Houston cannot afford to build anything less than a great Museum of Natural History. That or nothing.

VII The HISTORICAL SEMINAR: its OUTER SHELL and its INNER SPIRIT

*I*T IS easy . . . to outline a few external characteristics of the seminary," wrote Herbert Baxter Adams in 1884, "but difficult to picture its inner life."[1] Since Adams wrote this, more than seventy years ago, a great deal of attention has been paid to the external characteristics, the outer shell, and not so much to the inner life and spirit of the historical seminar. I chose the subject inner life and spirit of the historical seminar. I chose the subject for this occasion because the seminar has played an important role in my own work. In discussing it with others, I gained the impression that there was something peculiar in my use of this instrument of graduate instruction; and had the results of my experiment been less satisfying, I might have concluded that what I had was no seminar at all.

Further investigation revealed that I was not quite as original, peculiar, or off-side as I first thought. What had seemed the outer shell soon came to appear as the protective cover for the inner spirit where the vitality exists. My conclusion—which may be stated at the outset—is that the great seminars have been animated and made great not by any method but by the inner purpose, the great program, and the dominating idea of him who conducted it.

The seminar may be defined as a group of mature students or scholars studying and practicing the art of investigation and research under the direction of an experienced supervisor who sets the goal and sees to it that the best-known procedures are utilized by the group journeying toward it. The question arises as to what is the goal, the aim, of the director. What is he trying to do for these young people who have come for help? What, also, is he trying to do for himself? The answer to the question is simple: the director is trying to help these young people become historians. He, the master craftsman, is trying to make master craftsmen out of apprentices and journeymen. Years ago I read a story of a German *meister* of the craft of making beer kegs. The master often reminded his apprentices that in his own apprenticeship he made a perfect beer keg. He doubted that any of them would ever make a beer keg as perfect as his had been. He harried them, drove them; he cajoled and bullied them; and in the end the poor apprentices were quite full of beer kegs, and a little tired of the subject. And in time they probably learned that the master's beer keg was not as flawless as he had represented it. But this parallel between making beer kegs and making seminar papers will not be further developed here.

The director of the seminar puts the apprentices through the motions that the historian must make in the production of a finished work. He has them read, collect, analyze, organize; he has them write a paper with preface, outline, notes, and bibliography, and finally present the results of their labor—their own little beer kegs—for the judgment of the master and of their fellows. If there is no aim other than

84

this, then the seminar is a thinly disguised course in pedagogy, the director is conducting a trade school in historical mechanics, and the seminar is overrated, with more space in the graduate curriculum than its importance justifies.

Those who have glorified this sort of seminar have put great stress on the use of documents and original sources. Traditionally here is a place where the last shade of meaning is squeezed out of an official document. There is nothing wrong in putting a document under the microscope or through the critical wringer, analyzing it, looking into the bias and prejudice of him who wrote it. Nor is there anything wrong in seeking the motives of those who have committed great crimes or performed great services. The ability to do these things is possessed by many people, notably constitutional lawyers, probate judges, and police officers. These skills and critical attitudes can be taught in high school, and have been; they are taught again in college; they should be perfected by any student who has an M.A. degree. In the graduate seminar no student should receive any credit for having them, but should be penalized if he lacks them. These things—mechanics, procedures, and methods—constitute the outer shell, the indispensable minimum equipment needed by the student to qualify for admission to the sort of seminar that I am trying to delineate.

This brings me to the second question: What is the director of the seminar trying to do for himself? The answer is that he is trying to push out the bounds of knowledge. He has got far enough to ask questions, to know what kind to ask, but he has not found the answers. Therefore he calls in a group of graduate students, already equipped with method, takes them as junior partners, and sets them off on the quest for the answers to his questions. He is seeking aid while giving it. It is his hope that one out of ten will strike a trail, pursue it until he makes a field of inquiry his own, and become transformed into a creative historian. The director knows that he is a gambler, gambling in human possibilities, gambling that out of ten technicians there may emerge one who glimpses an idea and in pursuit of it becomes a master. The other nine will be no worse technicians than they were, and some of them may be a little better for having had pointed out to them a far country which they will never enter. That far country, reserved for the few, is the goal of the director. It has been the goal of all directors of all great seminars. Such seminars have been conducted by curious, restless investigators, bold enough to build a program of inquiry and writing around a compelling idea. With such men, and such men only, is found the inner spirit of the seminar.

In this paper I shall review briefly the origin of the seminar in Europe and its importation to this country and some results—good and bad—of its application in both places. Second, I shall show by example that the great seminars have been given by men with great ideas, men who used the seminar as an instrument of investigation. In the third place, I shall relate my own experience with the seminar.

It is generally stated that Leopold von Ranke of Germany was the father of the historical seminar, and it is assumed that he invented or adopted a new method of pursuing historical investigation. The method was already old, and had long been used in philology and in Biblical study. Ranke borrowed it from philology and carried it over into history, applying it to modern official documents rather than to ancient writs.[2] He was contemporary with Lyell, Wallace, Darwin, and Renan, who were applying the analytical and critical method with startling results in their respective fields. He turned the lecture room into a laboratory, using documents instead of a "bushel of clams." He was trying to make history a science, which has turned out to be as simple as making science history, something the scientists have had too much gumption to attempt.

Ranke's emphasis on documents came at a fortunate time in just the right place and was applied to a favorable

86

period, the sixteenth and seventeenth centuries. Situated in Central Europe, he was surrounded by new national states and others in the process of formation, and in each capital were the accumulated official records as yet untouched by historians. Ranke led the way in cracking these treasure houses to set numerous students off on careers of writing national history based on official documents in an era when the volume of official documents was manageable.[3] The documents were mainly political, and the histories based on them became almost entirely so. Ranke and his followers accepted Edward A. Freeman's dictum that "history is past politics and politics is present history" before Freeman phrased it. By such procedure, Ranke believed history could be written *wie es eigentlich gewesen ist,* but we know better now.

Ranke's method was accepted as a sort of historical Geiger counter, and students flocked to Berlin to acquire this new gadget. The results in two countries, Germany and the United States, are worth notice.

In Germany, Ranke built up a school—known as the German School—which numbered not less than thirty historians who attained in their day a considerable reputation, and many of them were distinguished. Most famous among them were Wilhelm von Giesebrecht, George Waitz, and Heinrich von Sybel. Their concern with official documents gave them the official view, and they began to tend more and more toward a glorification of the state. Sybel broke away from Ranke, and with the aid of Friedrich Dahlmann founded the Prussian school, which numbered among its members Johann Gustav Droysen and the notorious Heinrich von Treitschke. What they taught by Ranke's method we learned in 1914 and rehearsed in 1941. The study of state documents had led to the worship of the state. Ranke cannot be blamed for this perversion, although it grew naturally out of his basic principle, his belief that by depending on official documents one would arrive at truth as it really is. The Prussian school took the documents and proved to the satisfaction of themselves and many others that the German Empire was the noblest work of political evolution, that Prussia was the crown piece of the Empire, and that the Nordic race, of which Germans were the purest example, was superior to all others.[4] Nothing could better illustrate the danger inherent in any method considered infallible.

The results in the United States were not so fatal. While Ranke was at the height of his power, just before and after the Civil War, Americans began to go to Berlin and other centers, and return to the United States to preach the documentary gospel. They brought back the shell, the idea that they must be scientific, prove every statement with a footnote, that a felicitous style was no longer desirable—nay, it was reprehensible—that imagination was dangerous, too thrilling for the pick and shovel brigade of historians. They brought the method but forgot the substance; they brought what was valuable and needed, but some of them—not all—left behind what was indispensable, something Ranke himself had. They did what disciples often do; they warped and distorted the best work of the master.

These returning natives arrived on the American scene at a fortunate time, in the midst of an educational boom when new states were setting up new universities, when history as a university study was new. In 1880 there were only eleven professors of history in the whole country.[5] Any man who had the prestige of a European degree, and especially a German degree, could get a job. In 1884, these men took the lead in organizing the American Historical Association, and elected Leopold von Ranke the sole honorary life member. Eleven years later, Edward G. Bourne read a paper before the Association commemorating the hundredth anniversary of his birth.[6]

The cult spread and the newly trained Ph.D.'s took their Geiger counters into the state and national archives to repeat two generations later what Ranke and his men had done in Europe. They extracted the documents, mainly political, and began to turn out source books of all kinds. The movement culminated when Albert Bushnell Hart launched the *American Nation Series* in 1904, and to use his own words, drove a team of twenty-four historians through the field of American history. These volumes were fairly uniform in style, uniformly dull, heavily documented, primarily political, highly factual, wholly uninspired, and completely divorced from the reading public. In them was none of the savage beauty of Parkman, the insight of Macaulay, the vision of Gibbon, or the restrained yet luminous imagination of Jules Michelet, of whom James Westfall Thompson said: "He not only took history for life, he lived himself into the past to an extent unexcelled before or since."[7] Here was American history with all the blood and guts squeezed out of it. Something that had lived and moved was chopped up into twenty-seven parts so that some 280 years of history could be treated in ten-year blocks. These books had neither the charm of literature nor the exactness of science, and the series is being discarded in favor of a new one equally ephemeral. The conclusion seems to be that in this field of history the method of "science" confers no more immortality than other methods. There is no such thing as immortal history, a way of saying that there is in history no permanent truth; the facts may be permanent, but their meanings are in flux, and the historians only guess at them.

We have witnessed here the results of the seminar in Germany and the United States. The Germans perverted its use with such skill that they led their country down the road to destruction. When the Americans followed the method without imbibing the spirit, they bored the public to extinction. In the land of its origin, the method led to the devil; in the land of its adoption, to dullness. A mighty venture is now on to recapture the lost readers. Almost 100,000 people have indicated their willingness to try *American Heritage*. The editors have received some three-quarter million dollars as evidence that the people can read. Their present anxiety is whether the historians can write.

89

My second point is this: the great seminars that have most influenced historical writing have been given by men with great ideas. These men have shared their ideas and their programs with their students and used the seminar as an instrument for expanding the idea and executing a program. They have used any and all methods, but the exclusive use of any one method, even a "scientific" one, has proved fatal.

The best analogue to the seminar I am talking about is an exploring party bound for an unknown country. At the head of the expedition is the leader, the one on whom success is likely to depend and on whom blame for failure will inevitably fall. This leader has that which makes him the leader— that is, an idea of distinction. He does not know that he can reach it, or the nature of the obstacles in the way, or what it will be like when he does reach it, but the idea dominates him and makes him hazard the risk.

He selects carefully from those who volunteer for the adventure, hoping that each has intelligence, skill, and endurance. He calls the crew around him and speaks to them in this wise:

> You have engaged voluntarily to go with me into a strange and unknown country. You understand that I am not leading you through a park or meadow to show you trails which will, if you follow them, bring you home. I am leading you where there are no trails; we go to blaze a trail that others may follow. I know the direction but I do not know the way; I know the destination I hope we may reach, have an idea of what we will find there, but I am not sure of anything. I know that we shall pass over high mountains and penetrate dark valleys, that we shall see many new vistas, and even though we do not find what we seek, we will find something—an experience to remember all the days of our lives. One more thing I have to say: We are in this expedition together. The idea is mine, and as I share it with you, I want you to share what you find and what you make out of it with us. The campfire will be the clearing house for all.

The director is the leader with the idea of destination, the seminar members are the crew of axe-men, observers, hunters and scouts, front, flank, and rear. The library is the

90

high mountain and the forested valley where inspiring views and depressing confusion alternate. The seminar table is the campfire where the party gathers and each member reports what he has seen and what he thinks about it.

The essential elements of the sort of seminar I am talking about are two: the man and the idea. The important moment in the life of the man is the moment when this idea arrives to possess him and guide his work for a lifetime. In this moment he sees some pattern of truth, real meaning in the miscellaneous facts he has been gathering, and he knows that he has found something neither borrowed nor stolen, something his very own. It is the idea that transforms the mechanic, imitator, or pedant into a creative scholar with a destination and a purpose. The insatiable curiosity as to where the idea leads drives him to prodigious industry and endows him with an energy he never before knew. When the man, the prepared scholar, has received this idea he is ready to become the director of the sort of seminar where students enlist to go on a journey full of adventure and misadventure into an unknown country.

I have used the words "creative historian" and "creative seminar," words which I trust make nobody flinch. Those who do might turn to the etymology of *seminar*. In suggesting this I lay myself open to the charge of redundancy in placing the adjective *creative* before the noun *seminar,* which basically means creativeness. The seminar in this country was first called a seminary, but that term has been released to those less concerned with so profane a subject as history. Seminary and seminar stem from the French, *seminarius,* from Latin *seminarium,* pertaining to seed. Seminal comes from French and Latin *seminalis,* French *semen,* again pertaining to or consisting of seed, source, first principle, germinal, originative. There is nothing in the etymology signifying method or manner. Arthur P. Newton, the British historian of the Empire, thus defined it: "A Seminar (i.e., a bed in which to *sow* the seeds of intellectual effort), is . . . a group of disciples (I don't like the word *disciple* at all) gathered around a Master and inspired by him in a common field of inquiry."[8] If anybody wants to use the seminar in a creative manner, he will be on clear ground semantically.

Since the idea is so important in the seminar, I want to discuss that exciting moment when the idea arrives; when the idea and the man unite to transform an undifferentiated learner into a dynamic scholar.

Leopold von Ranke's name is synonymous with the "scientific" historical method, but I have never heard anyone speak of his basic idea, his main purpose, or the amazing program of investigation that he carried on for sixty years, resulting in fifty published volumes. He was not an imaginative man; he seemed to evolve slowly from his first task based on a compact body of documents through the history of the popes and of the national states of Europe, culminating his work with a World History, which he completed shortly before his death. One might think he never had that fine moment of insight to set him off on his course and give direction to all he did. I find evidence that he did have that moment, and that it came to him at the age of thirty. In February, 1825, he wrote to his brother: "I am now studying later modern history. Would I might be a Moses in this desert to strike and bring forth the water which is certainly there."[9] Surely here was a man making ready to set off into a desert—a desert of documents—to see if he could emulate Moses in the act of creation. Since he was working with documents, a documentary method was the natural one, incidental to his purpose and materials. "Der Stoff brachte die Form mit sich," he said in commenting on the Venetian papers.[10] The stuff not only determines the form, but it often determines the method.

That Ranke used his seminar to further his program is clear from the following passage:[11]

> I am still astonished at the talent and application of the young men who gathered around me. . . In this circle the work throve. We came upon the *Chronicon Corbeiense*, whose spuri-

ousness I first recognized without being able to prove it. The members of the seminar made the investigation which proved its falseness.

As we leave Ranke, I would like to pose this question: What made him in his day the leading historian of the world? Was it primarily because of the method he taught or was it because of the vast program he carried out?

Other men have been clearer than Ranke in nailing down the moment of synthesis spoken of by Fustel de Coulanges,[12] the moment of insight which transforms the student with a head full of inert knowledge into a dynamic scholar with a destination. Augustin Thierry spoke of this moment which led to his *History of the Conquest of the English by the Normans.*[13]

> One day [he said] when reading attentively some chapters in Hume, I was struck with a thought which appeared to me a ray of light, and closing the book, I cried, "All this dates from a conquest; there is a conquest at the bottom." Instantly I conceived the project of remaking the history of the English Revolutions by considering them from this new point of view.

Thierry describes the ecstasy with which one who has had this moment of synthesis works. He said that he devoured many pages to extract a single phrase or a word, and in the process, he said,

> my eyes acquired a faculty which astonishes me, and for which I cannot account; that of reading, as it were, by intuition, and of falling almost immediately on the passage that ought to have interest for me. . . . In the species of ecstasy which absorbed all my internal faculties . . . I had no consciousness of what passed around me. . . . The officials of the library and curious visitors came and went through the hall; I heard nothing, I saw nothing;—I saw only the apparitions called up in my soul by what I read.

But of all the accounts of how an idea, an obsession if you prefer, transforms a man, that of Heinrich Schliemann, who excavated Troy and the tombs of Mycenae, is to me the most remarkable. Schliemann was not exactly a historian, never had a seminar nor taught one, but had he done so it would have been a good one. His inspiration did not come in a flash, but had its beginnings, as is often the case, in early childhood, when he conceived the idea of finding the lost city of Troy and excavating it.

> If I begin this book with my autobiography [he wrote], it is not from any feeling of vanity, but from a desire to show how the work of my later life has been the natural consequence of the impressions I received in my earliest childhood, and that, so to say, the pick axe and spade for the excavation of Troy and the royal tombs of Mycenae were both forged and sharpened in the little German village in which I passed eight years of my earliest childhood.

The chain of events which made him one of the most original scholars of the modern world had its origin, not in a document, but in pure legend of his home village, a legend of buried treasure. In a pond near his home, legend said, each midnight a maiden rose from the water bearing a silver bowl; in a nearby burial ground a robber knight had buried his child in a golden cradle; and in the garden of the village proprietor other treasures were hidden underground. "My faith in the existence of these treasures was so great," said Schliemann, "that, whenever I heard my father complain of his poverty, I always expressed my astonishment that he did not dig up the silver bowl or the golden cradle, and so become rich." This was my first step.

The second step came on Christmas Day, 1829, when the eight-year-old boy received his father's present, Georg Ludwig Jerrer's *Universal History*, published the year before. In the book was a picture of the massive walls of Troy, but Schliemann's father told him that the picture was an imagination, that no trace of Troy existed, that none knew its location. This the boy could not believe.

> "Father," I retorted, "If such walls once existed, they cannot possibly have been completely destroyed; vast ruins of them must still remain, but they are hidden away by the dust of ages." He maintained the contrary, whilst I remained firm in my opinion, and at last we both agreed that I would one day excavate Troy.

The third step came at the age of sixteen when Schliemann was clerking in Theodore Huckstadt's grocery store, where one day a drunken sailor entered reciting the Homer he had learned before being expelled from the gymnasium for bad conduct. Schliemann says:

> He recited about a hundred lines of the poet, observing the rhythmic cadence of the verses. Although I did not understand a syllable, the melodious sound of the words made a deep impression on me, and I wept bitter tears at my unhappy fate. Three times over did I get him to repeat those divine verses, rewarding his trouble with three glasses of whisky, which I bought with the few pence that made up my whole fortune. From that moment I never ceased to pray God that by His grace I might yet have the happiness of learning Greek.

By the time he was ready to excavate Troy he had mastered English, French, Dutch, Spanish, Italian, Portuguese, Russian, Polish, Modern Greek, Ancient Greek, Latin, and Arabic—thirteen languages in all.

The fourth step came five years later when, at the age of twenty-one, the youth landed as a shipwrecked cabin boy to become a clerk in Amsterdam at £32 a year, half of which he spent on his studies. He knew it would take money to excavate Troy. There were no great foundations like those around which we timid scholars now flutter like candle flies; and had there been such, he would have stood no chance for a grant. Therefore, he made the money with which to excavate Troy. In another twenty-one years, at the age of forty-two, he retired as indigo merchant to Russia and gold merchant to the mines of California with a fortune. He wrote:

> Heaven continued to bless all my mercantile undertakings in a wonderful manner, so that at the end of 1863 I found myself in possession of a fortune such as my ambition had never ventured to aspire to. But in the bustle of business I never forgot Troy or the agreement I had made with my father . . . to excavate it. I loved money indeed, but solely as means of realizing this great idea of my life.

Five more years passed before Schliemann got to Troy, and then, between 1868 and his death in 1890, he not only found and excavated the lost city of Troy, but also Ithaca, Mycenae, Orchomenus, and Tyrus.[14]

This story illustrates the power of an idea followed by resolution to overcome and burn down all obstructions between the owner and his goal.

Let us now look at some American historians who conducted seminars, and try to determine whether they became notable because they followed a method or an idea. It is often stated that the first seminar was given by Henry Adams at Harvard, but this is an error. The first seminar was given by Charles Kendall Adams at the University of Michigan in 1869 when Henry P. Tappan was president.[15] I have found little record of what went on in this seminar or of its results.

The case is different with Henry Adams at Harvard, where he was an assistant professor from 1870 to 1877. It is quite easy to attribute all his merit to the fact that Adams spent some time in school in Germany, and to the fiction that he there learned how to conduct a seminar and became a great historian because he had mastered the latest wrinkle in German method.

An Adams is never a favorable witness for any Adams, but if we can trust Henry's own testimony, he never attended a seminar, knew little about history, and had no use for method. Here he tells of his activities after reaching Berlin in 1858:[16]

> Within a day or two he [Henry Adams] was running about with the rest to beer-cellars and music-halls and dance-rooms, smoking bad tobacco, drinking poor beer, and eating sauerkraut and sausages as though he knew no better. This was easy. . . . The trouble came when he asked for the education he was promised. His friends took him to be registered as a student of the university . . . and they led him to his first lecture.
>
> His first lecture was his last. The young man was not very quick . . ., but he needed no more than one hour to satisfy him that he had made another failure in education, this time a fatal one. . . . He had thought Harvard College a torpid school,

but it was instinct with life compared with all that he could see of the University of Berlin. The German students were strange animals, but their professors were beyond pay. The mental attitude of the university was not of the American world.

Instead of continuing in the university, Adams entered the gynasium, which he spoke of as a public school attended by boys of thirteen. He described this experience as a horror, and the school as "something very near an indictable nuisance." In the spring he left for good, and here is his description of his farewell: "He realized what a nightmare he had suffered, and he made up his mind that, wherever else he might . . . seek for education, it should not be again in Berlin."[17] He further stated that "he had revolted at the American school and university; he had instantly rejected the German university; and as his last experience in education he tried the German high school. The experiment was hazardous."[18] Of the university he said: "Neither the method nor the matter nor the manner could profit an American education."[19]

On his return to the United States after the Civil War, Adams found a gap of a thousand years—the medieval period—open at Harvard. President Charles W. Eliot gave him the job against his wishes and at four dollars a day. He said that "when he took his chair and looked the scholars in the face, he had given, as far as he could remember, an hour, more or less, to the Middle Ages."[20]

It is interesting to know what procedure Adams, the most nearly perfect American historian, followed. He has told us in these words:[21]

> He frankly acted on the principle that a teacher, who knew nothing of his subject, should not pretend to teach his scholars what he did not know, but should join them in trying to find the best way of learning it. The rather pretentious name of historical method was sometimes given to this process of instruction, but the name smacked of German pedagogy, and a young professor who respected neither history nor method, his sole object of interest was his students' minds, fell into trouble enough without adding to it a German parentage. . . .

97

Nothing is easier to teach than historical method, but, when learned, it has little use.

Adams said he selected as his victims a half-dozen intelligent boys and started them reading whatever they pleased as a background for law. There must have been something about Adams that touched them off, for, he says:[22]

> The boys worked like rabbits, and dug holes all over the field of archaic society; no difficulty stopped them; unknown languages yielded before their attack, and customary law became familiar as the police court; undoubtedly they learned, after a fashion, to chase an idea, like a hare, through as dense a thicket of obscure facts as they are likely to meet at the bar; but their teacher knew that his wonderful method led nowhere.

In view of this evidence, and it is a primary source however unreliable, no one can attribute Adams' greatness, as a conductor of a seminar or as historian, to methodology or to German training. I have not found that the self-depreciatory Adams ever admitted that he had that moment of illumination which determined the way he would go. The only obsession he admitted was the futile pursuit of an education.

Though something called a seminar had been given at Michigan and at Harvard, the institutionalization of this device in this country occurred at Johns Hopkins. Here, in 1876, was established a real university as distinguished from such colleges as Yale, Princeton, and Harvard, fortunate in that it was not cluttered up with undergraduates. Johns Hopkins was a graduate school from the beginning, the only one then worthy of the name. Its reception amazed its founders; its instantaneous success astonished all. Of it Sidney Lanier, in his "Ode to Johns Hopkins," said:

> *So quick she bloomed, she seemed to bloom at birth,*
> *Fore-seen, wise-plann'd pure child of thought and pain,*
> *Leapt our Minerva from a mortal brain.*

A more prosaic writer has said: "To look through the list of first students at the Johns Hopkins University is to obtain a preview of the men who were to become the distinguished

98

members of the faculties of American universities in the thirty or forty years that followed."[23] Within ten years, sixty-nine men had received the Ph.D. degree, and all but thirteen had positions in thirty-two universities. Among the early fellows are such names as Walter Hines Page, Charles Lane Poor, John H. Latane, Herbert Baxter Adams, John Spencer Bassett, W. W. Willoughby, Josiah Royce, John Dewey, and Woodrow Wilson.

The mortal brain that launched this educational meteor was Daniel Coit Gilman, the first president. That he thought men of ideas should outrank men of methods is made pretty clear in his statement of purpose:

> It misses its aim if it produces learned pedants, or simple artisans, or cunning sophists, or pretentious practitioners. Its purpose is not so much to impart knowledge to the pupils as to whet the appetite, exhibit methods, develop powers, strengthen judgment, and invigorate the intellectual and moral forces.

Again he said:[24]

> In forming all these plans we must beware lest we are led away from our foundations; lest we make our schools technical instead of liberal and impart a knowledge of methods rather than of principles. If we make this mistake we may have an excellent *polytechnicum*, but not a *university*.

The first historical seminar was set up at Johns Hopkins by Austin Scott at the time George Bancroft was writing his *History of the Formation of the Constitution of the United States,* published in 1881. Scott was acting as Bancroft's assistant, and the seminar was put to work on the problem. I quote Herbert Baxter Adams:[25]

> The seminary had the feeling that they had been admitted to Mr. Bancroft's workshop, and that, by the examination of his materials and his methods, they were being taught the art of constructing history. The very manuscripts which Dr. Scott had prepared while collecting and sifting facts for Mr. Bancroft, were shown to the seminary. Questions still unsolved were submitted to Johns Hopkins students for their consideration, in company with their instructor. . . . The feeling was thus engen-

dered that, in some slight ways, the seminary was contributing to the great volume of United States history.

Here again we see the students assisting the director on a real program of scholarship.

In 1876, Herbert Baxter Adams returned to America with a Heidelberg Ph.D., and became one of the first fellows at Johns Hopkins. I suspect that the seminar he later established would rank at the top in terms of what came out of it. His first idea was to continue to study the Roman and German origins of community life, but this soon proved to be impracticable, and he turned to American Institutional History. His students ranged far and wide over the United States, writing about American institutions.

Need I follow the careers of Edward Channing and John Bach McMaster and answer the questions as to why students flocked to their seminars and considered it something to remember that they had studied with such men? Was it their methods or their prodigious program of work that made these men worth while? Need I answer the same question for the man from Portage, Wisconsin? Did he come back from Johns Hopkins to send his name and influence around the world because he had learned mechanics or because he, by looking at his own rude environment, had hit upon a seminal idea which fascinated those who worked with him and set many off on quests to the frontier to create a school of thought?

In 1901, Herbert E. Bolton, a recent graduate from the University of Wisconsin, was exiled to the province of Texas to teach elementary history to the reluctant sons of cowboys. He brought no idea with him, but picked one up on the borderland he had entered, where Anglo-American met Latin-American, English met Spanish, Protestant met Catholic. The archives were at hand, but he could not use them because he knew no Spanish. Deciding to devote himself to the Spanish borderlands, he studied Spanish under Miss Lilia Casis and set to work. He later went to California where he inspired, and sometimes made a little dizzy, his many disciples who have filled the chairs of Latin-American history all over the continent and beyond. In addition, he turned out a volume of work, which if not prodigious, is quite respectable.[26]

Another Californian had a somewhat similar idea long before Bolton. Hubert Howe Bancroft, like Schliemann, Walter Leaf, George Grote, and James Ford Rhodes, took time out to make money before turning historian.[27] The regular guild like to depreciate Bancroft because of his method, that of hiring better-trained historians than he was and paying them with the money he knew how to make. Thus he got the title of Clio Incorporated. He never had a seminar, never studied method, but he evolved a compelling and expanding idea which would give him no rest. Though historians are reluctant to admit him to the guild, they must concede that he put the scholarly world into his debt, and that his books, with all their faults, will outlive the *American Nation Series,* old and new.[28]

In all these examples from Leopold von Ranke and Henry Adams to Herbert Bolton and H. H. Bancroft, we find one common denominator. It is not a method, but the presence of an idea or an obsession which creates a driving energy and an insatiable curiosity. In each case where the seminar was used by these men, it was used as a creative instrument to assist the director in extending the area of knowledge.

I speak now of my own experience with the seminar. In my entire life I have had only two ideas which I consider to have any originality. I am here tonight because I followed those ideas, without much regard for method, using that which would facilitate the pursuit. Each idea has resulted in a book. A new seminar was organized around each idea shortly after its arrival, maintained until the book was published, and then abandoned. No idea, no seminar.

The first idea, embalmed in *The Great Plains,* came on a stormy night in February while I was reading in preparation of an article about the Texas Rangers for a magazine sponsored by a crooked oil company intent on fleecing the public.

I was writing the article for three reasons: I knew something about the Texas Rangers; I was on an instructor's salary; and the crooked oil company paid well until it was rudely interfered with by a United States marshal. Months of research preceded the exciting incident of that night, the moment of insight and synthesis when the miscellaneous facts I had gathered formed a pattern, fell into place, and took on meaning, that moment when something triggers the mind loaded with what Toynbee calls inert knowledge, and brings understanding.

The Colt revolver, which had often been used as a precipitant, always the favorite weapon of the Texas Rangers, was the grain around which the idea formed. I suddenly saw the six-shooter as the natural weapon of the man on horseback, of men moving in an open treeless country where there was grass for horses and cattle and room in which to ride. I saw that in weapons a revolutionary change took place where men left the wooded country and entered the treeless land, where men mounted horses to do their traveling, their fighting, and their work. I had as yet practically no proof of what I knew, but I found it shortly and in abundance, and wrote the story of the historical significance of the six-shooter—I called it the American revolver—which was accepted by *Scribner's Magazine* before I had ever taken a seminar.

But more important than that, I now had a bigger question to ask: What other changes took place where men left the forest to dwell on the plains? Nobody could answer that question which had not been asked before, but the question would not go away, and I had to go to work and answer it myself. The big question broke up into smaller ones. Where timber and grass meet, what change took place in geology? What in botany? In zoology? In anthropology? What in the laws of land and water? What in literature? Having specialized in history, I lacked education, knew neither geology, nor botany, nor zoology, little anthropology, nothing of law, and not much more of literature. Hitherto I would have been ap-

102

palled had anyone suggested that I explore these formidable subjects. Yet my curiosity about these suspected changes was such that it acted like a fire to burn away the obstacle of complete ignorance. I studied all these subjects insofar as they threw light on the questions. Geology and law came hardest, but were quite rewarding.

Because of that quest I understand what Thierry meant when he spoke of the ecstasy of search, of being insensitive to what went on around him, and of reading as by intuition. I could read for my purpose a dozen books a day, and it came to the point where anything pertaining to the Great Plains would jump out of the page at a glance, just as Thierry described.

I was authorized to offer a course on the Great Plains. I did not rate a seminar, and I did not know enough to lecture. I said to the class: I think something important happened to ideas and institutions when men left the woodland to live on the plains in middle America. Will you help me find out what happened to this and that and the other? I surreptitiously converted this class, and succeeding ones, into a seminar—into hunting answers to my quesions. My students were good hunters. As Henry Adams said, they scurried about like rabbits; they dug holes all over the Great Plains.

It is difficult to remember how much I stole from them, but I cannot forget that I stole something. One student described the Great Plains as a strange land where the wind draws the water and the cows cut the wood. Another explained the collapse of the early farming settlements by saying that in the East civilization stood on three legs—land, water, and timber. In the West, two of these legs were withdrawn, and civilization was left to stand, or topple, on one leg. I took that.

There is evidence that the students got from me and from their fellows something in exchange for what they brought, an understanding of the significance of things hitherto without meaning. This evidence comes in letters containing newspaper clippings on subjects we explored. Students sent specimens of barbed wire, pictures of windmills, and occasionally an old six-shooter. Though nearly twenty-five years have passed since the seminar ceased, the letters and specimens still come.

About ten years elapsed between the stormy February night when the apparition appeared and the hot July day when the book was published. Practically nothing but the *Scribner* article was published in that long interval. Fortunately, I was in Texas, where the ideals of high-pressure scholarship had not then obtruded. Nobody told me I ought to produce, write articles, get in print whether I had anything to say or not.[29] I had time to mature what I was about, to do what I had been preparing for since I was carried to the sun-blistered plains of West Texas at the age of four, and where I saw at an impressionable age everything that is in the book except Indians and irrigation. The Indians had just departed, and the water was never there.

The second idea, of greater magnitude but less originality than the first, came to me one spring morning in 1936, and like the first it came when I was working on something not closely related to it—another case of serendipity. Two years later I organized a seminar around the idea, and fourteen years still later the seminar ended with the publication of a book. The central question this time was: What effect did the uncovering of three new continents around 1500 have on the civilization that discovered and for a time owned the continents? Again the central question broke up into specific ones. How did the sudden acquisition and subsequent development of all this new land affect the individual? How did it affect such institutions as absolutism, democracy, slavery, and religious polity? Did it do anything to economic practice and theory? Thirteen years elapsed between the time the idea came and the time I began to write, years of alternating exaltation and misery. Avenues of inquiry radiated in all directions, to new stars in a new hemisphere of astronomy, to the botanical gardens in Europe, to seekers after windfalls of New World gold and silver or hides and fur, to the ensuing booms and bubbles, and to the economic theories and political philosophies that men made to rationalize an unseen revolution.

The young people who joined me on this expedition contributed much to the final result. Their minds were fresh, often they were eager, and they explored far and near. One question I asked was how piracy of the sixteenth to the nineteenth century was related to the frontier. Why did it arise shortly after the frontier opened? Why did it end early in the nineteenth century? Why was it centered in the Caribbean? Three successive students were assigned the subject. The first two returned with nothing—just a passable paper on pirates· but the third found something. Piracy, he said, had headquarters in the Caribbean because the precious metals from the mines of the Great Frontier had to pass that way en route to Europe. Spain owned the mines and would allow no other power in the Caribbean, a closed sea. No nation could break the monopoly. The alternative was to wink at and support all pirates who preyed on Spanish commerce. This England, France, and Holland did, sharing with the buccaneers their good fortune but never their bad. Finally, Spain's monopoly was broken. Pirates were no longer an asset to anybody; all nations turned on them, and their day was over. In the seminar I had spoken of the entrance to the New World symbolically as a golden door. This student suggested, rather shyly, but with some insight, that the subtitle of his essay on pirates might well be "The Thief at the Golden Door." Thus did he wrap his thesis up in a phrase. I have never asked the experts whether we had a proper seminar. I know we traveled together to far places, we worked at exciting tasks, and I think we came to know what Francis M. Cornford meant when he spoke of a "silent, reasonable world, where the only action is thought, and thought is free from fear," and we traveled in "the company of clean, humorous intellect."[29]

VIII   The UNIVERSITY HISTORIANS and HISTORY TEACHERS

*T*HE MOST commendable thing about this program, aside from the papers just read, is the fact that the American Historical Association has seen fit to give some attention to the phalanx of unknown persons who are teaching history, or its substitutes, in the public schools of America. The Executive Secretary, Dr. Boyd Shafer, says in his current report: "Last year we reported that the Ford Foundation had granted $148,000 for our Service Center for Teachers. That center, directed by Dr. George Carson, is now in operation, preparing pamphlets on the content of high school history courses and annotated lists of books for history teachers, as well as providing consultant services when requested." It is quite likely that this interest on our part will continue as long as the $148,000 lasts.

Those who made this program did not assign a specific topic to each of the speakers. All were asked to comment on the subject: "Historians and the Teaching of History." The language can be interpreted in many ways. Are we to talk about historians as teachers of history? Who are the historians anyway? Are they those who warm chairs in universities? Are college teachers of history historians or are they mere history teachers? Is there a hierarchy of university wholesalers, college brokers and high school retailers of this intellectual commodity? Does teaching in a university make me a historian? Does teaching in a high school keep me from being a historian? These mean questions came to me as I looked at the language of this subject in my more malignant mood. In better temper I decided that I would discuss the relation existing, at least in some places, between history teachers in state universities and teachers of history in the public schools, mainly high schools. I have had some experience in both the high schools and in a state university, but I am not acquainted with the parochial schools, and only to a limited extent with the colleges. My observations are based primarily on the situation that exists in my own state between the University and the teachers of history in the public schools. I am assuming that a somewhat similar situation obtains in other states.

In practically all the states excepting a few on the eastern seaboard, the state university is the leading educational institution. It is the seat of the graduate school, it has the largest enrollment, it is the place where many teachers are trained, where most are trained who go beyond the B.A. degree. Since this university is supported entirely by the state, it owes a real obligation to the state, and it escapes this obligation in the long range at its peril. Each such university has a school of education which undertakes to prepare teachers for the public and other schools by requiring courses in the methods of teaching. Under the leadership of what may be called the Columbia philosophy, these schools of education have expanded their curriculum and proliferated their courses in an extreme manner, and have in places approached monopoly control of the public school system. This perversion has gone

107

so far as to create a reaction. In history this reaction is represented by the philippics of Professor Bestor and the creation by the American Historical Association of the Service Center. In general it is represented by the book "Why Johnnie Can't Read" and by a cartoon showing a wailing child shouting in indignation: "I don't want to express myself. I want to learn to read."

The progressive educators were so successful in capturing the public schools that they drove a wedge between the teachers of subject courses, such as history, and the methodologists, between the arts and science college and the public schools. About forty years ago the universities set out to improve standards in the high schools. They sent out inspectors to see that standards were met, demanded a certain proportion of college graduates, and suggested revision of the course of study before the high school could be classed as affiliated, before its graduates could enter the University without condition or examination. The function of affiliation has now been taken over by the State Department of Public Instruction which is likely to be staffed by those fresh out of the school of education whose dean writes the new laws for the Superintendent. No longer is a professor of history invited to visit a certain school to see if history is being taught in an adequate manner by competent people. As a matter of fact, history was practically abandoned, and something called social studies substituted in its place. In social studies it seems that the crayfish method was adopted, that is, you begin with the present and go backwards, hoping that you would eventually get to Greece or Rome. In the course of three years one bright boy visited the water works seven times to get oriented, an object lesson in adjusted, integrated, correlated and duplicated community living.

If in the attempt to explain the gulf that has grown up between the university historians and the teachers of history in the high schools, I have placed all the blame on the progressive educationalists, it is because I got to them first. They are mainly responsible, but the university is not entirely blameless. Its main fault is that it did not adjust to the changed situation. Faculty members resented the change, grumbled about lowered standards, but took no further action. They accepted what was done. In effect they abdicated and retired to the cloister, a little relieved to be rid of responsibility for what went on in the public schools. Of course they would not admit this, but in their hearts they feel that it is true. The teacher in the public school was no longer our business.

When this story began, forty years ago, state universities were almost solely undergraduate institutions. The end product then was the B.A. graduate, and the whole faculty had their eyes concentrated on him. They got him a job, they kept in touch with him, they rejoiced in his success as an extension of their own and put the blame for his failure where it belonged. In the interval the university grew and the graduate school was created to give the M.A. and eventually the Ph.D. Every faculty member wanted to get into the graduate school where the classes were smaller, the work load less, the honor more and the salary bigger. The focus of the collective faculty eye was no longer on the B.A. candidate, but on the M.A. or the Ph.D. who was going to the newly created state colleges or the more recent junior colleges. The B.A. who went to teach history in the high school was no longer important to Professor X. He was left to the professional educator with most of his instruction in history in the hands of graduate students, part time teachers. This fact led a parent, who had professors, to remark that his son was a senior before he ever saw a professor. Today there is little doubt that freshmen and sophomores are better taught in the state colleges than they are in the large state universities.

With the rise of the graduate school there came the emphasis on research. This research took the form of writing, and the writing had to be printed in a learned journal before it could be marked A. No longer is the instructor or assistant professor promoted because he is a good teacher; he is promoted because he had turned out ten articles and fifteen book reviews in two years, and had a book in progress. All aspirants must have a book in progress. What interest does the teacher of history at Schulenburg or Dime Box have for the university historian who was busy mucking up footnotes?

In the beginning, forty years ago, the young instructor may have been informed that it would be to his interest to be a scholar, to write something if he had something to say. Of late years he is told to write something whether he has anything to say or not. Administrators discovered the "up-and-out rule." I believe it was invented in Harvard, and it has been applied in state universities more savagely than in Harvard which can make allowances. Young people have to produce or get out! Without production one could never hope to reach that haven of permanence, the Associate Professorship.

Here we come to the crux of the business. For whom does the university historian produce? Is it for his students? Is it for the teacher who is working his heart out in a nearby town? Not at all. He is producing for his peers—and his superiors. He is playing the big checkerboard with its forty-eight states. Since he is already in *The* university, there is nothing else for him in his own state. He is playing to Kansas, Nebraska, Arkansas, Louisiana, California, Michigan, and he may even dream of others too precious to mention. Nothing could be of less interest to him than the teacher of history in the high schools. He is faced away from them, not towards them.

There is another factor that operates to keep the university historian separated from the teachers of history within the state. That is the policy of recruiting almost exclusively from outside the state and even outside the region. Many state universities actually seem to have an inferiority complex. They feel that somehow one of their own graduates is hardly qualified to teach in *The* university. If one is co-opted, he has to work about twice as hard as the one from a distance

110

to gain equal recognition. To this I can testify. Of course inbreeding can be very bad, and should be used with discrimination. I have taught in two universities notable for its practice! One is Harvard and the other is Oxford. But a little line breeding is not bad when you want to render service to the state, to the people who are paying the bills.

State universities are packed with people who are in the state but not of it. They have no interest in it, no concern with the problems of the people who are not their people. In this sense, as a friend of mine pointed out, faculty people are comparable to the army, to the army officers who move from one place to another but never grow into any corner of the land. In some cases the attitude is almost hostile. If you doubt this, try suggesting to a committee of a university faculty that a concerted attack be made on some problem of interest to the people of the state. They shy off and retire into polite silence. From such people teachers in the public schools cannot expect too much. They cannot really expect anything except instruction in the classroom.

The point I am making is that state university faculties are not very much interested in the problems of the people in the states wherein they work. University faculties are not much interested in how subjects are taught in the high school. Let me illustrate this with something that occurred in relation to my appearance on this program.

The University of Texas has a fund from which to pay the transportation expense of faculty members who are on the programs of learned societies. The regulations provide that the individual must have his name on the program for a paper which is the result of his own research. Now I knew that this paper did not require much research such as I have proved I can do, but the officials of the American Historical Association rather insisted that I accept the assignment. At the suggestion of the chairman of the department, I sent my application to a committee which determines whether we walk or ride to these meetings. This committee is composed of a chemist, chairman, psychologist, a linguist, a musician, English, educationalist, engineer, dean and botanist. A representative group. There was a suspicious delay in the answer; I suspected that my application was being denied, and wrote the chairman the following letter:

December 15, 1956

Gentlemen:

Several days ago I sent a request for travel expense to your committee. The basis for this request is that I am scheduled to address the American Historical Association in St. Louis on problems pertaining to history as taught in the public high schools. I have not heard from the committee, and have a feeling that my request may be rejected because of the nature of the subject I am to discuss.

Actually I am not much concerned with the financial side of the question, but I am concerned with the principle involved, namely the attitude of a State University towards the public schools. Therefore I would like to request, if my application is rejected for any reason other than lack of funds, that the reason be given to me in writing before the holidays.

The American Historical Association is exerting itself in many directions to improve the history offerings in the public schools of this country, and it probably will be deeply interested in the position taken by the colleges and universities, particularly state supported institutions, towards this problem.

Very truly yours,
Walter P. Webb

Garrison Hall 102

I had not received an answer to my letter when I left for this meeting, but I did receive a copy of a letter, dated December 14, addressed to the Dean of the College and of the Graduate School. It reads:

December 14, 1956

Dear Sirs:

The Committee on Attendance at Meetings of Learned Societies at its meeting on December 13 considered an application for a travel grant from Professor W. P. Webb to present a paper entitled "Historians and the Teaching of History" before the Service Center of Teachers of the American Historical Association meeting in St. Louis on December 30, 1956.

The Committee felt that this application did not come within the area of presentation of original research for which grants should be approved. The Committee was unanimous in its opinion that it was in the interest of The University that Professor Webb present this paper and accordingly voted to inform the appropriate administrative officials of its action and to request that efforts be made to find funds from which a travel grant could be given to Professor Webb for presentation of this paper.

Sincerely yours,

I am sure the committee will argue that it is restricted by law, but I suspect that the ruling comes from interpretation. Now let me do some interpreting. Had I been on any section of this program other than one concerned with teaching, with teachers, this application would have been approved. I could have read a paper on the irrigation possibilities of the Jordan River in Utah or on the mathematical chances of paying the national debt from a tax on the gambling tables of Las Vegas and it probably would have been approved. But I was to talk on the vulgar subject of teachers. I was to talk about what the State of Texas had paid me to talk about all my life, and I even hoped to go back to Texas with some of that $148,000 put up by the Ford Foundation. I would use the money to improve the relations between The University of Texas and the people who support it. If I may judge by what I have seen, we'll need the whole amount. And while 1 am interpreting, I'll make another. And it is that of the eight members on the committee, at least seven are from without the state. I would have better than a Las Vegas chance to win.

The History Department at the University of Texas is belatedly taking steps to reestablish some relation between the historians and the teachers of history. Fortunately an enlightened dean is supporting the move, has taken the initiative in it. He has told the department that if we do not accept the task of reestablishing this relationship, it will be taken over by another division of the University which I need not name. He has agreed to provide funds for the employment of a competent person who will devote half time to the task.

I think I am being fair when I say that the department members as a whole have accepted the suggestion of the dean with some misgiving. Their reluctance is understandable because for twenty years they have not been called on to render any service directly to the public schools. They are out of practice. In a staff of about eighteen permanent members, not more than three have ever taught in a high school in Texas. Only one of these is under 60. It is doubtful if during the past twenty years more than two have ever been present at any history section meeting of the State Teachers' Association. The closest connection we have is through the Junior Historians, an organization supported by the Texas State Historical Association which is directed by a member of the faculty and supported by the University. Of the eighteen members of the staff thirteen are from other states. Excepting the director of the Junior Historians it is doubtful if the whole staff could name ten teachers of history in the high schools of Texas. If we exclude the five natives, it is doubtful if the remainder of the staff could name two. The one they could name is a Ph.D. who has been unable to get a job in a college. In view of the facts and the guesses presented above, it is easy to understand the reluctance of the historians to have in the department someone who will be concerned with the teachers of history.

I have attempted to list below some of the thinking about this person.

1. There is no member in the department, granting competence, who should be asked to give up his career, quit playing to the big checkerboard, and bury himself in service to the state.

2. The man brought in would have to be good enough to be acceptable as a regular member of the department. Is it possible for a man who devotes himself to high school history teachers to be that good?

3. Assuming that such a man could be found, what would be the psychological effect on him of working with a group of real historians? Would he feel that he lacks the

114

prestige in the group? Would he ever be admitted to the graduate faculty? Would the budget council recommend him for advance in salary?

On the other hand the following questions may have occurred to some: If the man appointed is a strong man, would he build up strong support in the state that would make him troublesome? Would he destroy the splendid isolation? Would we be introducing into the bosom of the department the viper of professional pedagogism?

I have necessarily had to discuss my own university and my own department in this analysis. I dare say that the situation in Texas exists to some extent in many other state universities because universities have much in common. I apologize to my colleagues for undertaking to say what they think and what they know about the subject.

In conclusion I wish to summarize what I have said and close by suggesting a setup that might enable the historians in the universities to reestablish contact with the teachers of history in the high schools.

First, I explained how over the last forty years the various departments in the university have become separated from contact with the teachers in the high schools. This separation was attributed to two things: (1) The virtual capture of the public school system by the professional educationalists; (2) The rise of the graduate school which shifted the attention of the faculty to upper-level work with emphasis on research and writing. This shift has taken place in state universities despite the fact that they are still primarily undergraduate institutions. The instruction in high schools has deteriorated to such an extent as to create a reaction. An effort is now being made to find a remedy for a bad situation.

Now for the suggested setup that may bring that remedy:

1. The Department of History will select from within the department or from without a man who will devote at least half time to reestablishing the lost contact. He should

be trained in history; he should be acquainted with the state; he should have had experience in high school teaching. He should not be barred because he is a native.

2. The man appointed should realize what he is in for. He must not expect immediate enthusiastic support from his colleagues who are playing another game. He must be at first sufficient unto himself; determined to follow his own game. If his colleagues draw a circle to cut him out, he should draw one that will take them in. He should be a broker between his colleagues, the real historians, and the teachers of history in the high schools. At every opportunity, he should engage their services, arrange for them to be invited to the high schools to talk about medieval civilization, modern Europe, the War for Southern Independence—often called the Civil War—and Latin American culture. Above all he should not retire from the department or attempt to build a little empire of his own.

3. The man appointed should have the support of the administration until he proves himself one way or another. He should have a good salary, one that will make him respected and enable him to respect himself, and he should have advancement as he deserves it.

4. His duty would be to visit the high schools, talk to the history classes about history, get other departmental members to do the same. He should seek out the best history students and let them know that the university is interested in them. He should seek out the best history teachers, and arrange for groups of them to come to the university for conferences where they would meet the historians. If he were as good as he ought to be he would render a real service all around, to the department, to the better teachers and the better students of history in the high schools.

This paper which the Committee on Travel to Learned Societies did not deem worthy of $84.70 travel expense is long enough. We in Texas are now interested in doing something about the teaching of history. And I want Dr. Carson to keep this in mind when he comes to distribute that $148,000.

IX The WRITING of HISTORY in TEXAS

INCE I was ten years old I have been a reader. I remember well when I found that I was equipped to launch my own little boat into the wonderful sea of literature, when I set out to read something not in the school reader. Here was a wonderful world into which I could venture merely by following lines of type set down on paper. This first story I read was, I think, but I am not sure, in *The Baptist Standard,* and it was about a magic crow and a boy named Barney Bylow. The title, as I recall, was "Witch Crow and Barney Bylow." This crow had the power to grant any wish the boy might make, and what the boy wished was that he might always have some money, he didn't say how much. Instantly Witch Crow granted Barney Bylow his wish, and Barney found a penny—a single penny—in his hand. Now a penny wouldn't buy much, even in 1899, and Barney wanted more. But he could never have it. No matter how much Witch

Crow piled up in front of him, the moment he touched it, it was reduced to a single penny.

It was at this same period that I bought my first book; I should say acquired rather than bought, because I traded ten signatures from Arbuckle's Coffee packages for it. The book was entitled *Jack the Giant-Killer*. It was in big type on very slick paper; it had about twelve pages and the most garish illustrations, all blood red or pitch black, that you can imagine. Jack was an attractive lad, but the Giant looked awful as he pursued Jack in a dead heat with his knotty club. Fortunately, Jack scrambled up a wonderful beanstalk to temporary safety.

The love of reading soon led me to admire those remarkable people who wrote it. Surely these writers must be the chosen of God, so great that they must all now be dead. How could ordinary, living people put down words on paper in such a way as to transport the reader to the stars above or cast him into the pit below? Would it be possible for me ever to do anything like that? I doubted it, but I desired it with painful intensity. Two incidents will illustrate.

At about the age of fourteen I read "The King of the Golden River." While still under the spell of it, I confided to my father that if I could write something like that I would be willing to die. My father was a very practical man, and I recall his shocked expression that I should entertain such an impractical and improbable idea. He might have encouraged me a little, but he did not because to him such a notion seemed no more than juvenile foolishness.

Four years later I was teaching in a country school and as some of you may recall, we were then required to attend a three-day teachers' institute, held at Christmas time. The idea of the authorities was that we would be professionally improved; our own idea was that we could engage in a little courtship unsupervised by our pupils and patrons. This courtship idea was incentive enough, but on this occasion I had an additional one. One of the speakers at the institute had written a book, and I had never yet seen a man or woman who had written a book. I could hardly believe, even then, that such great ones could possibly still be alive. In my mind I built up a portrait of a god-like creature who would be as distinguished looking as Ralph Waldo Emerson's picture. I was never more disappointed in my life. When this author finally came on the stage, I could hardly believe my eyes. He was about five feet, four, weighed about 120 pounds, and the only author-like feature I could notice was a scraggly beard no thicker than an American Indian could grow. I had simply oversold myself on the appearance of authors. I now know a great many authors, but not more than one or two who come up to my early idea of what an author ought to look like. In fact, on more than one occasion I have been told that I don't look like an author either.

I relate these personal incidents to show how far Texas has come in respect to authors since I became conscious of them nearly sixty years ago. Now they are everywhere, not confined as they once were to New England or Old England. It is probable that today Texas and Texans are turning out more books each year than any two New England states, and it may be turning out more than all of them together. The Texas Institute of Letters is a sort of association of Texas authors consisting of about 100 members, all of whom must have produced one or more books. Here in Corpus Christi is the headquarters for the Southwestern Writers' Conference. When it meets once a year the hotel is filled to capacity with real and would-be authors, and even with publishers from far and near who come to see what they can pick up.

Within the past month I have had come to my desk the following books by Texas authors. Tom Lea's *The King Ranch,* George Fuermann's *Reluctant Empire,* Hubert Mewhinney's *A Manual for Neanderthal,* Ramon Adams, *The Best of the American Cowboy,* and Charles Carver, *Brann and the Iconoclast,* not to mention two books by the authors we are here to honor today. In addition, I have read manuscripts of two forthcoming books on the Alamo and a book on contemporary Texas. If I would go back into 1956 I would have to add Fred Gipson's *Old Yeller,* Will Tom Carpenter's *Lucky 7,* and Joe Frantz's *The American Cowboy.* Three presses within the area, two in Texas, are busy turning out Texas books. They are Naylor of San Antonio, the new University of Texas Press in Austin and the University of Oklahoma Press at Norman, Oklahoma. One literary magazine, *The Southwest Review,* is published by Southern Methodist University and another magazine of high intellectual quality, *The Texas Quarterly,* will be launched by The University of Texas early next year.

I was instructed to speak fifteen minutes on the general subject of history writing in Texas. All the books I have mentioned above are history books to me, though most of the authors are not professional historians. To me there is no better history of the small boy in the Hill Country, in West Texas, than Fred Gipson's *Old Yeller* and *The Home Place* and there is no better picture of the Texas trifler of forty years ago than Blackie Scantlin in *Hound Dog Man.* Tom Lea's *The King Ranch* and Paul Horgan's *The Great River: The Rio Grande* are notable historical works by a fiction writer and artist. Charles Carver's *Brann the Iconoclast,* a book you will hear much about, is the history of what a firebrand could do in a conservative community like Waco. It is the exciting story of one of the most remarkable six-shooter battles in all the West, the only gun battle on record in which all participants were killed.

In the realm of sober history, Texas has a long record. Among the early historians are Henderson Yoakum, Homer S. Thrall and Dudley G. Wooten who devoted themselves to the history of the state. With the establishment of The University of Texas in 1883, we enter the era of the academic historians. The first among these was George P. Garrison, followed by the most eminent Dr. Eugene C. Barker, historian of the revolution and biographer of Stephen F. Austin. Today there are some eighty graduate students at the University alone going through an apprenticeship in historical writing, and there are many in other institutions.

Corpus Christi and Del Mar College are doing something very fine in honoring two authors who are carrying on the tradition of historical writing. These two authors are very fortunate in living in a community that is conscious of what they have done. It often happens that an author is almost unknown, and is scarcely noticed by his home community. In 1931 I published a book entitled *The Great Plains*. It was my first book and I was thrilled by the prospect that my neighbors and friends might take note of it and be impressed. The first review, by one of my colleagues, was the most damaging that the book received. A year later the editor of the local paper called by phone late at night and our conversation went like this:

"Are you the man that wrote a book called *The Great Plains?*"

"Yes, I wrote it."

"We have a wire from New York saying that it has been awarded the Loubat Prize."

"The Loubat Prize?" I said. "I never heard of the Loubat Prize."

"Well," he said, "don't feel bad about that. I never heard of the book."

Just recently George Fuermann of Houston published what I consider a very remarkable book, *Reluctant Empire*, a history of contemporary Texas. This book is mature in many respects. It is an attempt to analyze Texas today. The reviews outside of Houston praise the book highly, but those written by Mr. Fuermann's neighbors and friends are highly critical or downright hostile. Often the attitude of the neighbors seems to be that "*that* man could not possibly write a *good* book."

It is difficult for those who have not written a book to know how the man who has written one feels about it. He feels about it somewhat as a woman who has had a baby feels about it. The writing of a book is quite analogous to the having of a baby as I understand it. There is the same pride of creation, the same tender care and solicitation, maybe the same blindness to its qualities of loveliness and intelligence. Everybody ought to understand it, appreciate it, and ignore its few faults. Any reviewer who takes liberties with it is a lowdown skunk, a jealous skunk at that.

Nobody has better described the pangs of bookmaking than Gilbert Highet in his volume, just out, entitled *Talents & Geniuses*. Read his chapter on "The Birth of a Book."

There is quite a contrast between the two books whose authors are honored here today. The span between Dallas in the 1950's and the last seven years of George Washington's life is a considerable span indeed. Between these two extremes lies an enormous field in which historians engage in a work as varied as the life of the nation is varied. The life of Dallas and the life of George Washington are but two colored threads in the tapestry of American history. Every person, community, state and institution between George Washington in 1793–1799 and Dallas in 1950–1957 had a history, but little of it has been written. There are some notable gaps to be filled in.

In Texas the most notable gap includes Corpus Christi and the whole Gulf coast. Because I am a teacher, I am always pointing out things that people haven't done or things they ought to do. Because I am something of a writer, I am always trying to get others to write what I would like to write, to have a book, to fill a gap. This Texas Gulf coast is a gap that ought to be filled. We Texans have written much about the land, the Indians, the cowboys, the oil fields, but we have written practically nothing about the 750 mile salt water edge of Texas. We have ignored the Gulf, the Golden Crescent, and the strange life of those who live on the edge of the Texas sea. There is as yet no literature about it, and scarcely any history.

Not long ago there was placed in my hands the most

exciting manuscript that I have ever examined. I doubt that anyone in this audience ever heard of it, though it was written in less than forty miles of this place and about the exciting life that goes on in the villages and communities that form a necklace along the Texas shore. This manuscript may be literature; it certainly is history. It fits in to the great gap that exists in the Texas story.

In 1924 a little woman from Michigan went to Florida on vacation. There she met a tall and rugged young man, a professional fisherman and guide. He gave her a whirlwind courtship, married her, and took her to live in a palmetto shack on a sand spit known as Mud Key. Four years later this couple came to Corpus Christi, to Aransas Pass, and finally to Port Aransas, another sand spit of which Padre Island is the most famous. Here on these islands from Port Aransas to Port Isabel this couple lived and took their living from the sea. They became famous, especially in that insane segment of society known as fishermen. The big man knew all about fish, where they were, where they were going to be tomorrow; he seemed to know what fish thought about.

Some two years ago this little woman began to think back on what she and her fishing genius had been through in thirty-two years. She sat down and wrote the story of their experience in storm, disaster and occasional triumph. She tells how they built their home at Port Aransas and again at Port Isabel with what they fished from the sea, everything in the house except the windows. She wrote as a real writer must, without inhibition, of adventure, the hardship, of how he once ran away and how she once ran away, setting off from this very town in a silver bus into a strange world that she had had forgot, the world of land. She makes it clear that it is not always easy to be the wife of a genius, but she stuck and shared his whole strange life. She set out consciously to etch his character but in doing so she unconsciously etched her own.

George E. Roberts, better known as Florida Roberts, lies

today with a fatal illness in a hospital in this city. It took some persuasion on my part to induce Elda May Roberts, his wife, to come with me to this meeting so that she could see that authors are human, and I want Dr. Howard and Dr. Carroll and others to see that all authors do not come out of colleges and universities. Occasionally one comes straight out of life. For fear that Mrs. Roberts may run away, I am going to ask her to stand up before she does.

Since I would expect all of you here to buy these books, I shall not interfere by telling you much of what is in them. Dr. James Howard has given us a contemporary portrait of a Texas city. He has undertaken to explain why Dallas has become a great city, second in size, first in fashion, and a hard contender for first place in finance, distribution and things cultural. Dr. Howard's book is a solo performance. He did it without connection with any group of working historians, and with very little financial assistance.

Dr. John Alexander Carroll worked in a different tradition. His subject pertains to Texas only in that George Washington belongs to us all. He and his collaborator, Mary Wells Ashworth, not only had the privilege of working on the greatest American, but they had the privilege of working with one of the greatest biographers and American historians of our time, the late Douglas Southall Freeman. More than that, they found themselves confronted with the obligation to complete the great work that he had begun. They wrote the final volume in the seven-volume biography of the first President of the United States. It was a tremendous responsibility executed with commendable skill.

Since authors take much of their pay in appreciation, and since that is the pay they treasure most, and since it is often very slow pay in the author's own community, I want especially to commend Del Mar College and Corpus Christi for paying so generously and promptly its faculty members who have done so much to reflect honor on the institution and the town.

124

X The UNIVERSITY PROFESSOR
and the SOCIAL STUDIES

M Y SUBJECT is the relation of the University Professor of History to his subject and to those he instructs in the subject. We can understand him better if we ask—and answer—the following questions. What is the University Professor of History trying to do? What are his main objectives? How does he go about attaining them? What, in short, does he have to do to get and to hold by merit the rank of professor in a *real* University?

By definition a real university is a place where scholars are assembled and assigned the double task of discovering knowledge and of teaching others how to acquire and perhaps discover knowledge for themselves. It is important, if we are to understand why the University professor acts as he does, that his role is a dual one. He is a discoverer and he is a teacher. In the public schools, and to some extent in the colleges, a person is expected to be a teacher only. Nothing more is required of him. By being a good teacher, and being reasonably mindful of the conventions, he can attain tenure, be promoted to the highest rank, and finally be retired with a long dinner in the Commons and a piece in the local paper. The University Professor, unless he takes refuge in administration, can hope as a teacher for very few of these rewards. As an exceptional teacher he may, after some debate, attain tenure, be promoted with more debate, but he will never attain the high rank or the high salary—things which in a real university are in theory reserved for him who has also been a discoverer.

Here we get into some academic jargon, to describe these academic discoverers. What the University Professor is supposed to do is to pull the cover off some hitherto unseen or unknown truth. He makes a written record of what he has found, or thinks he has found, publishes it in a magazine, or book, often in such style that few will read it. This is research, this is production, this is the coin of the academic realm. This is what brings the university professor prestige, offers from other universities, invitations to national or international congresses, all of which are reported to the administration which is counting upon him or cutting notches on his record. As the notches accumulate, he shoots upward, hoping to fall into a well-upholstered endowed chair. The important point is that in such a meteoric rise teaching plays practically no part. It is assumed that if he is a *master* of knowledge he can impart it, an assumption not yet completely disproved.

Now we may return to the original question: What is the University Professor of History trying to do? Naturally, he is trying to get to the top of the profession. He wants to be a discoverer, a research man, a producer; his eyes are fixed on that high rank, high salary, the endowed chair. He knows he will never get there by teaching alone. He must do more than that.

I am talking here about focus, the point on which the main emphasis is placed in a real university. In the public school emphasis is on teaching, in the college it is mixed, in the university—the real university—it is on research. I might add here that this system is in a sense self-adjusting. For example, if a high school teacher becomes a writer, as well as a teacher, that teacher is likely to be called to a college; if a college teacher made some notable discovery, that teacher would almost certainly be drafted into a university. As the English express it, he would be co-opted, brought in to the corporation of scholars.

We have recently become concerned here in Texas, and in other states as well, at the width of the gap that has opened up between the teachers of history in the public schools and the professors of history in the university and the colleges. This meeting, sponsored by the American Historical Association, the college at San Marcos, and The University of Texas is evidence of that concern. We are now engaged in a joint effort to bridge that gap in so far as it can be done. My remarks will be limited to the situation existing between The University of Texas and the Public Schools of Texas.

The University of Texas aspires to be a real university. It has always put the emphasis on securing scholars of distinction, real discoverers, for its faculty. It pays a premium for them. About thirty years ago it established the graduate school and began to grant the Ph.D. degree. It undertook to train people to staff the numerous colleges that were growing up in Texas and elsewhere. It divided the faculty into two categories, designating one as the graduate faculty and—as far as I know—not designating the other at all—just faculty. The requirements for admission to the graduate faculty are quite rigid.

Prior to the establishment of the Graduate School, the faculty of the University were very close to the teachers in the public schools. The public schools were then in process of being affiliated and faculty members were often sent out to inspect classes in history, English and math, classes being taught by recent B.A. graduates. At that time the public schools offered about the only outlet for the teachers that were being

127

turned out at the University. The history professor in the University knew what the history teacher in Temple, Taylor and Tyler was doing.

Suddenly the bond was broken.

The State Department of Education took from the University the right to grant affiliation. Now agents from the Department of Education made the inspection, visited the schools, and not professors from the University.

Then, as already stated, the University created the Graduate School, set up the graduate faculty and began to prepare people for college jobs. The professor of history now wanted to be a graduate professor. He wanted to handle graduate students who were fewer in number, less rebellious in nature, and often quite helpful in forwarding his research. He got special credit for a number of M.A.'s and Ph.D.'s he directed, but nothing special for the B.A.'s. The B.A.'s now came to have the status of a Congressman at large, they did not belong to anybody. Not so with the M.A.'s, less so with the Ph.D.'s. They belonged to the professor and he was most solicitous of them. He helped them get, not high school jobs, but college jobs, and he kept in close contact with them. I suspect that the members of the graduate faculty of The University of Texas could give the name and the present position of every former student whose dissertation he directed. I doubt that all of them together could give the name and present position of a dozen B.A. or M.A. students who are teaching history in the high schools. On the other side, I wonder how many high school teachers could name five history professors now on the staff, much less have any knowledge of the great discoveries they have made and recorded in the last five years. I am not criticizing either group but pointing out that their neglect is both mutual and reciprocal.

During these thirty years something worth noting has happened in the field of high school history teaching. The Texas State Teachers Association abolished the history section in the annual meetings. I am not sure, but I think I presided over the last one. I got called to The University of Texas because of a paper on history teaching which I read before this section in Corpus Christi over which Professor Duncalf of the University history staff presided. I was brought to the University to teach a course in the teaching of history so it would not be given by somebody who knew no history, but knew how it ought to be taught. I edited *The History Teachers Bulletin* until it ceased publication. In short, I abdicated along with the others.

Last fall I accompanied Professor James Taylor to Houston where he was scheduled to make a talk before the members of this organization. When I went into the room, the attendant handed me a program, and I scanned it to see what was there about history. As I recalled, there was exactly nothing. The term history did not appear in the program. As far as I could tell history had been abolished.

After the meeting I hurried to Miss Myrtle Roberts to see if my worst fears were to be confirmed.

"Miss Roberts," I said, "what on earth has happened to history in the public schools? I don't see it mentioned on this program. Has it been wiped out completely?"

Miss Roberts was very consoling. "No, Mr. Webb," she said. "It's taught like it always was; they just changed the name."

Since I grew up they have changed the name of a lot of things, such as undertaker, appendicitis, catarrh and Spanish influenza. I suppose all these changes have come to make normally unpleasant things more tolerable. History never struck me as having unpleasant connotations. It has endured since "Omer struck his bloomin' lyre" a thousand years before Christ and will endure as long as human beings are curious about the past. I am a little curious about the genius who changed the name, but I can guarantee that no historian from the University had any part in it, another evidence of the gap that has come to exist.

At any rate here we are and here you are. As yet we have

no idea of what the teachers of history in the public schools are willing to do to narrow the gap, to get acquainted again. There are a few things that university professors would like to do to reestablish connection.

We would like to get reacquainted. We need to understand what your problems are in order that we may know better how to deal with the students you send to us.

We believe that in the realm of scholarship we might on the proper occasion have something to offer that would be of use to you and to your students. A scholar is inclined to be generous with the treasures he has dug up through his research. He really likes to talk about them, to share them with others. It might be worth while for your students to hear from a man who knows all about medieval architecture, the southern plantation life, or some of the things (selected) that went on around the Court of Louis XIV. Every high school is within easy driving distance of some college or university where these special scholars live. Find out what they are doing by inviting them in when there is no football game.

We are particularly interested in the students in your classes who have a talent for history. We may be able to encourage them with a word, which means much to the young, cite them to good books, to good college teachers.

Because I like to write, I am always on the lookout for those who have a talent for writing, a feeling for words, a gift for the telling phrase. I really want students who will write books, not those who are willing to stop with themes, theses and dissertations.

It may not be easy to bridge a gap between two groups that have different functions. There is a common bond, devotion to the subject and desire to serve best those who like to pursue it. Each can perform his function better by knowing what the other is doing.

XI   The ART of HISTORICAL WRITING

J TAKE it that I have been invited to appear on this program for no other reason than that I have written four books and some magazine articles. The assumption must be that I am a writer, that I know something about writing that those who have done less of it do not know, that I *can* impart to others what I know, and that others can listen to me and learn *from me* to do the sort of writing that I have done. The first assumption, that I am a writer, may be true in a limited sense. The assumption that I know something is less true; the last two assumptions, that I can impart what I know, and that you can *learn* from me what I know are both false. I cannot impart what I know, and you who are my hearers cannot learn it from me. The road to writing is no less royal than the road to learning.

Even so, all of us who like to write love very much to hear others who like to write or have written talk about their own experiences. Out of the talk we gain encouragement, bolster the ego of the talker, and may occasionally pick up an idea or a trick or a principle that will be helpful.

I must first tell you what sort of writer I am not, and then I shall be free to speak of my experiences as the sort of writer I am. I am not a poet, or even a versefier. I undertook to write a poem once, but when I saw it later, after the fog had cleared away, I realized that I had chosen the worst possible means of attaining a desirable goal. I never again jeopardized a love affair with my poetry.

I must tell you in the second place that I am not a writer of fiction, though I have always wanted to be. I wrote four short stories, sold three, and gave one away. I was not good at making plots of my own, and I had scruples about stealing them, though I understand that the practice is common and often encouraged. Moreover, I could not handle feminine character—my women, like those of Eugene Manlove Rhodes, creaked when they walked, and neither I nor the editors could abide such travesty.

I will say that this desire to write fiction, and a love of reading it, has had, I think, some effect on the more pedestrian type of writing that I have done. In an effort to prepare to write fiction, I practiced the three forms of fiction writing, description, narration, and exposition. I also practiced writing conversation or dialogue, an extremely difficult thing to master. Also as a reader I was continually watching the author of the story I read to see how he worked his magic. In this manner I developed clarity and insight, style, more flexibility of paragraph and sentence and better diction than I would have had otherwise. My most useful adjunct to this sort of practice was the wastepaper basket. As I tried one form after another, I threw the sheets into the wastepaper basket where such sheets belong.

As things turned out I became a writer of history, and as you know, history is written mainly as narration and exposition. I suspect that I have a better mastery of exposition than

I have of the other forms.

There are many advantages in writing history, and I will mention some of them. The greatest one is that you have a tremendous amount of solid material on which to draw. All of the past is yours, all that man has thought, said or done. You as a historian are like a woodsman standing in a great forest with axe in hand, free to chop where he will. History is a good refuge for those of us who lack the talent and the imagination to spin the imaginative tales of a Maugham or Hemingway. Anybody who is industrious enough to read the books, turn over the original documents and intelligent enough to see cause and effect can write history. I must add, however, that talent and imagination do not hurt the historian if he has them. He does not have to write literature to be a historian, but many—and I might say—the best historians have written history that approaches literature.

Another disadvantage the historian labors under is that even if he has imagination he must stick to the truth as revealed by the sources. He must always work within the framework of truth, of what happened, who did it, when and where. He has no license to fabricate, to create dramatic situations, to make a faultless hero never seen in real life, or to picture the women of history in other than their own colors. Because he is so bound by the facts, he finds it more difficult for him to write in an interesting or absorbing manner than it is for the creative writer. The facts get in the way of imagination and act as a powerful restraint. His characters are not puppets who move at his command for the amusement or entertainment of the reader; they are wilful men and women who go about life with that strange and undramatic perversity of real human beings. They are as unmanageable as your own family.

It would seem that it would be easy for the historian to move from history to the more alluring realm of fiction. As some of you know, I have worked all my life in the field of Western American and frontier history. You also know that many writers of fiction—not necessarily creative writers—

have made a good income by writing western fiction. People have often said to me: You know all about the Texas Rangers, the Great Plains and the Great Frontier. Why don't you do a novel that would be a masterpiece? There are many reasons why I don't attempt that novel. The most important one is that I am too much the historian. The facts I know would intrude on the fancy I would have to have. I would pack the novel with too many facts, with too much history, so many facts and so much history that the editors would paper my walls with rejection slips. Editors are not as dumb as we may think. They know their readers, and they know that a reader will not stand for too much history. They want instead conversation, and if you expect to write fiction you had better master conversation.

I am not saying that successful writers are not students of history. Most of them are, and such history as they include had better be sound. But in the successful writer of fiction imagination must *dominate* the manuscript, and all else must be its garment, correct but never conspicuous.

Let us examine briefly the relation of the historian and the creative writer to the audience. The creative writer of high quality influences people by a dramatic presentation that appeals primarily to the emotions. He leads his reader to identify himself with the hero, suffer with him, triumph with him, and like him hate the villain. In this process the reader identifies himself with the *cause* for which the hero fought, and he makes it *his* cause. *Uncle Tom's Cabin* is perhaps the most notable example, but there are many others.

The historian offers his wares to the same people, but ordinarily has fewer purchasers. His approach is the intellectual one, and the implication seems to be that people have more emotion than they have intellect. The historian exerts his influence by giving people an *understanding* of their past and the world around them. The reader of history knows that he is being informed; the reader of fiction is being moved, often without realizing it.

134

I have tried my hand at writing history calculated to move people by giving them understanding. I have just published a small volume entitled "More Water for Texas" which was written to *disturb* the people of Texas by showing them that they face a water problem of such magnitude that all of us will suffer if the state and the nation do not act to capture the water now going to waste in the Gulf of Mexico. The facts set forth in this little volume are well known to all water engineers and to many others. My function as a historian was to take these same facts and present them in a way that more people could understand. I wanted all people to see that under our present practices, and by our present neglect, we are extending the desert by robbing the land of underground water and failing to save the surface water.

Another book calculated to appeal to people through their understanding is entitled *Divided We Stand*. This book divides this nation into three sections, the North, the South and the West. It shows by figures from the U.S. Census the way wealth is distributed in this country. It shows that the North has the lion's share, and that the people in the South and the West own very little. I can't give you details, but I can present the picture of wealth distribution, based on the census of 1930. At that time the North owned about $85.00 out of every hundred dollars in the land; the South and West divided the remaining $15.00 between them. But by way of contrast, the South and the West have about 85% of the natural resources, such as lumber, gold, silver, and petroleum— they have these resources *located* in their area, but most of the resources are *owned* and *controlled* by people in the North. I also pointed out how this concentration of wealth was brought about by one political party, a purely sectional party with nearly all its members in the North. The controls which concentrate the wealth of a great nation in one corner of it was brought about in the years following the Civil War when the South was disfranchised and the West not yet settled. Congress, made up almost entirely of Northern Republicans, passed the laws that made the concentration possible.

The facts I used in *Divided We Stand* are beyond dispute. They are available to everybody. My function was to simplify the problem, present the facts in a manner that people could grasp and understand.

It is my opinion that *Divided We Stand* is now out of date. The figures I used are those of 1930. I am now taking the same figures for 1950. It is my guess that in the two decades, from 1930 to 1950, the relative position of the people in the South and West was materially improved. However the figures turn out, I must use them. If they show that the South and the West lost ground—and they didn't have much to lose—under twenty years of democratic rule, then I shall change parties.

I wish now to speak of a book written around a single idea, one that presents a thesis. Many cautious people will tell you that a historian should never have a thesis, that he should just put down the facts. My own view is that he should *not* have a *bad* thesis. But if he has a good one, and makes it stand up, then he has something of distinction. I have written two books, each based on a single idea. *The Great Plains*, published in 1931, was the first; *The Great Frontier*, 1952, was the second. The central idea of *The Great Plains* is that the physical conditions of the American West are so different from those of the East, that a complete revolution in living was necessary for those people who left the well-watered eastern woodland and undertook to live in the naked wide spaces of the western plains. The writing of the book was a thrilling experience. Since I refer to it later, I shall pass on to *The Great Frontier*. I may say, however, that *The Great Plains* has been accepted as a sound interpretation of western American history.

The basic idea of *The Great Frontier* is that when Columbus and his associates discovered the continents and islands of a whole new world, they opened up a great frontier —the Great Frontier—to the people of western Europe. This great frontier exerted an influence on western civilization comparable to the influence exerted by the American frontier on American civilization. The main effect was that the sudden acquisition by Europeans of the immense wealth and resources of the Great Frontier precipitated a boom on western civilization that lasted as long as the frontier was open. The boom lasted from 1500 to 1900 or 1914. The frontier closed about 1900, and with it ended the boom and the set of conditions that accompanied it. The modern institutions and ideas with which we are now equipped had their origin and growth during the boom, are adapted to boom conditions, and were not seriously questioned as long as the boom lasted. Among these boom-born institutions are democracy, capitalism and free enterprise; among the ideas are those of progress, freedom and individualism. The problem that confronts all the people of the western world is that of a closed frontier, of adjusting their institutions and ideas to conditions today rather than those of yesterday.

My purpose in stating here the basic idea of these two books is to illustrate how a book may be written around a single idea, a thesis. In such case, the historian undertakes one of the most hazardous of enterprises, that of making an interpretation. What he tries to do as a writer is to get the reader to stand with him on the high peak of the basic concept and look at the world or the area from a new vantage point. He points out to the reader relationships he has seen, and gives illustrations from the past of his ideas. Some understand and agree; others disagree, often violently. Since absolute truth can never be found in history, the writer must exercise his greatest skill in exposition and narration in order that he may be understood.

I take it that most of you are too busy with the immediate to take the time required to work out a problem of such magnitude. It so happens that I am paid to do just that sort of thing and am furnished facilities in the form of library and research students. Though you may not have the time or the facilities to tackle the sort of academic idea as the two I have struggled with, you can nevertheless tackle the sort of idea that interests you. The problem is the same. I know of no better way to write a book than to have behind it some compelling idea that you wish to present. Such a central idea gives unity to your effort, inspiration to your industry, and it may result in a production that is both artistic and sound. This basic idea can become an obsession, make you a little crazy, as one must be to write a good book—a little crazy but not too crazy.

In conclusion, I am going to speak of the better experiences of a writer. All of you have had the delightful experience of writing a sentence or a passage that was for you just right. You feel that you have plumbed a new depth and unleashed a power of expression you didn't know you had. You have, to use an athletic expression, played over your own head.

Several years ago, I had a letter from Stanley Vestal asking me to say what in my opinion has helped or hindered good writing in the *Southwest.* In answering Vestal, I said some things about writing that I found very satisfactory when I read the letter. Here are some extracts from that letter:

April 5, 1945

Dear Mr. Campbell:

It is rather difficult for me to set down my ideas of writing as suggested in your inquiry. Much of what I would say is trite, well known to those of experience. Any discussion of factors helping or hindering writers would be mere verbiflage—a term recently coined by a student here. I do not know what they are, and I suspect they are different for each individual.

The basic requirement, in my opinion, for a writer is that one must have an inner and insatiable urge to express himself in words and sentences. A person with such an urge may be born in a southwest desert or a Mississippi swamp. It is this desire which drives the individual on to acquire the tools which will make him effective. He reads all he can get hold of, and he watches the tricks of the writers he reads to see how they obtain their effects. He attunes his ear, but rarely his tongue, for words, phrases, effective sentences, and he begins to strain his experiences and observations through his critical sifter to get effects. In time he begins to put something on paper—and what a labored process these first tentative steps are. He is plagued by untold inhibitions which block his path like weeds that choke a drainage ditch. It is only by treading the paths often that he can beat down the inhibitions and conquer the mere mechanisms of composition.

I now come to a factor which is as potent as it is intangible. I mean the ability of the writer to see that about which he writes, not as something in a book but as something which exists for him. He must be in his mind in direct contact without an intermediary. For example, if he is describing or giving a narration involving a horse, he must *know* the horse, not what somebody said about horses.

The nearest I ever came in achieving this immediacy of my subject was in writing *The Great Plains*. During that period of writing, about five months, people thought that I dwelt in a University office with a single window facing north. That was only where my body was, not myself. *I* was living for that whole time on the Plains. I was not living at any given place or time, but I was all over the Plains and I was in any period of time that was convenient. I was living in both spatial and time dimensions. I had built myself a Plains cocoon, and I dwelt within that cocoon to spin my tale, and everything not in that cocoon was not in my real world. Do I make myself clear? The only reason I am not a great writer is that I cannot find other suitable cocoons to dwell in. How I wish I could.

Why could I do this for the Plains? One reason is that I began to live there at the age of four, and throughout a sensitive and not very happy childhood I either experienced or observed practically everything described in the book. From there I passed into the world of books and finally gravitated to those dealing with the life I knew but did not as a child understand.

I would, if I could, say something about the subconscious and its role in the art of writing. There is no doubt that the great writer plumbs depths that he himself does not know he possesses or why. Once he gains an insight into something profound, he opens new chambers of power, of style, or knowledge which lie deeply submerged.

You may say that Webb is writing very subjectively. I know of no other way to write. Words can be put together objectively, but they have never made literature. I am not a great writer, among other reasons, because I dare not be subjective, to write inside-out, to tell all, to be shameless, to sacrifice my family, my place in a University faculty. I am not willing, and I was not willing as a youth when there was time, to live hard enough to store up experiences about which one can write. I was never willing to go broke, to get drunk, to hobo, to soil my hands in factories, to take ship to sea. Consequently I have had nothing, aside from the interpretation of the land of my childhood, to say. I am not a writer because I have lived too much with books and too little with life. The inner urge has been there since I was ten years old, but it was not strong enough or relentless enough to do the job.

Another thing a writer needs is leisure, and I do not mean merely the time to do unimportant things. I think I mean solitude, a sense of aloneness. Have you ever thought of the contributions prisons have made to greatness in thought and in literature? There is O. Henry, Luther, Machiavelli, John the Baptist (I am not too sure of him), Marco Polo, Ignatius Loyola, Robert Louis Stevenson, Prescott and Parkman, the historians and scores of invalids. Had Hitler not gone to prison he never would have written his damnable book which almost wrecked the world; had Roosevelt not had infantile paralysis he would never have gained the courage to undertake what he has undertaken. In conquering infantile paralysis, he conquered fear which is the greatest of all paralyzers, and left it behind him forever. Above all a writer must free himself from fear, especially from fear of University English departments and fear of violating academic standards.

Nothing I have said pertains particularly to the Southwest. The writer is not regional. He, like oil, is where you find him, but there is nothing in the Southwest to preclude him. The best literature thus far has been ranch literature. I think Andy Adams and Eugene Manlove Rhodes have produced some—by interpreting their own land. I can name no others among the dead who will live, and I am afraid I can name fewer among the living who will not die soon after their decease. None of us has been willing to pay the price, and neither have you nor I.

Sincerely yours,
Walter Prescott Webb

On Publishers Checks I wrote the following:

It is clear from the record I have set down that after my return to Texas, I began to make some money above my salary. This extra money came from the publishers and when it came it always seemed to me that it was money I had not earned. It was not like a gift, or finding money, or money won at poker or on the ponies. It was much better money, better even than a salary check. A publisher's check does something to me that no other check does, and I get more pleasure from a fifty dollar check from a publisher than I would from a hundred dollar check from any other source. There is so much behind a publisher's check. For one thing, there is mystery; you never know until you open the envelope whether it is large or small. It comes as a tribute to your power of idea, to your skill, art or industry. It comes because you have knocked down a lot of obstacles with your literary ball. You have done something that *made* a publisher sign a contract, something that will people out there spend their money, pay a small cash tribute to you in return for the privilege of examining your best thoughts. Perhaps they may admire your art, or your industry, and wish that they "could write something like that." Writing is like bowling. You send the literary ball down the alley, and you are a poor bowler indeed if you don't hit something; but occasionally you are feeling just right, the ball goes true and you knock down everything in sight. You make a ten strike, and the satisfaction you get out of it is out of all proportion to the importance of the event. You have a sense of power, of conquest, of succeeding at that you have always wanted to do. The publisher's check is proof that you have done it.

Best personal description. I was giving a summary of the presidents of the United States in this century. And this I did to Calvin Coolidge.

> Coolidge was probably the most provincial of all presidents, and so steeped in conservative tradition that he sought to change nothing. No leadership was asked of him, and he embarrassed no one by volunteering any. The only people he embarrassed were those who tried to get him to say something. Apparently he broke his health and brought himself to the grave prematurely by the intensity of his inactivity.

In giving the reasons for the decline of the Republican party which ushered in twenty years of democracy—and if that be treason make the most of it—I pointed out how in its days of triumph after the Civil War, the Republican party turned its back on the South, on the West, on labor, and on the farmer, relying for its strength more and more on business and more and more on big business. Then, in 1929, when all business collapsed, the Republican party had nothing left to stand on. In the debacle of failure the farmer, the laborer, and the small business man went over to the opposite party. I summed it up in one sentence by saying: "The Republican party quit the people long before the people quit the Republican party." I like that sentence so well that when I wrote it I quit work for the day.

In *The Great Frontier* I was dealing with the brutal realism of frontier or farm literature, trying to account for its appeal. I said:

> We are a people with a cow-lot background, such as Hamlin Garland sketches in "Up the Cooly." There is for us nothing new on the farm. We know it all intimately—the long hours, the sweaty, stinking, heavy underwear, the debt and the mortgage, the way it feels to drag in at twilight after a day in the field to sit on the doorstep and pull from our aching feet our brogan shoes before we eat the coarse evening meal.

In *The Great Frontier* I was again discussing literature, the effect that the closing of the frontier will have, is having, on literature. Of this end of an age, which we are now seeing, I wrote:

> The end of an age is always touched with sadness for those who lived it and those who loved it. That sadness is usually attended with much knowledge, some wisdom, and a sort of jaded sophistication. Neither knowledge nor wisdom brings happiness; more often they bring disillusionment. It would be very interesting to speculate on what the human imagination is going to do with a frontierless world where it must seek its inspiration in uniformity rather than in variety, in safety rather than in peril, in probing the harmless nuances of the known rather than the thundering uncertainties of unknown seas and continents. The dreamer, the poets, and the philosophers are after all but instruments which make vocal and articulate the hopes and aspirations and the fears of a people.
>
> And so, as we linger in contemplation of the great tapestry of modern literature which has left us images of what the human imagination did with a New World, we know that it represents a special kind of experience, that it is done, and our last impression as we turn away is that to many of us it was as big as God.

XII   The TEACHERS and WRITERS
of HISTORY

$\mathcal{J}$N THE letters I received preliminary to my appearance here my correspondents were careful to inform me that I was supposed to talk to history teachers about teaching history, with stress on this art as practiced in the high schools. They knew that I am connected with a large university, and they were telling me in the polite language used habitually by school people, that they hoped I would deal with reality and not with some fine-spun theory developed and hermetically sealed in academic chambers. Even in this introduction the speaker has commented on my position, my office in the American Historical Association, on the fact that I have written books. This sort of talk is likely to cause you to wonder just what I know about the problems and trials of the high school teacher who for six hours or more a day teaches five classes, makes two to four different preparations, and substitutes for the parent, the preacher, and the policeman in managing anywhere from 75 to 125 young—well, what shall we call them? Some are lovesick, some want to be outlaws, some want to develop their muscles, and a few desire to develop their brains. But one thing they all have in common, and that is the fears, doubts and frustrations of adolescence—things which make problems for teachers. Certainly it is easy for a university professor who teaches six hours a week instead of six hours a day to give teachers a lot of good useless advice. But don't be fooled by what you have heard about me. As a teacher I have been over the whole road, from the one-teacher school where I taught thirty classes to an English university where I was supposed to teach twenty-eight classes in a period of nine months, but didn't because the students did not always turn up. I started this career in the country, more than half a century ago, and I started so far up the creek that if I had been any farther I would have been over the divide. I may have forgotten some of the anxieties that plague the teacher in the public schools, but I remember enough to still feel that at times the task seems beyond endurance. For years after I got into university work, my recurring nightmare was a roomful of freckle-faced ninth graders in history completely out of control. I relate this personal experience to reassure you that my knowledge of public school teaching, though now out of date, is not wholly theoretical. I may add one other personal note. I taught history three years, each year in a bigger if not better high school, and was called to the University to give a course in the teaching of history so that the course would not be given by another department that knew little history.

Even though I may now have convinced you that I once knew something about teaching history in high school, I am sure some of you are curious as to why this sudden burst of interest on the part of university professors on the problem of public school teachers. It is no secret that this interest is something new, and it needs some explaining. I am going to attempt that explanation.

144

My explanation will be divided into three parts:

1. How the program got started.
2. How and why the problem we are dealing with arose.
3. What has been done on the program in one state.

1. How the Program Got Started

This program got started when the American Historical Association secured a grant of $148,000 from the Ford Foundation to found the Service Center for Teachers of History. This act of the professional historians—by which is meant primarily university and college professors of history —indicates that the historians felt the compulsion to do something about the teaching of history in the high schools and in the elementary schools. Here they draw, consciously or unconsciously, a distinction between historians and history teachers. I do not like this distinction, but it has its usefulness.

The historians, that is the American Historical Association, chose Dr. George B. Carson, formerly of Chicago, as Director of the Service Center for Teachers. In an article in *Social Education* for February, 1957, Dr. Carson stated the purpose of the American Historical Association in launching this program. He said:

> "The Association believes that its best contribution to improvement of the teaching of history is to try to bridge the *growing gap*, which results from increasing specialization, between teachers of history in schools and specialists in historical research in universities."

The term, Service Center for Teachers, deserves attention. Service Center for Teachers—every word needs emphasis— Service Center—for teachers. What service does this Center give to Teachers? I list three things:

a. It has employed a group of specialists to prepare helpful bibliographies and to write monographs on certain topics that need to be taught and emphasized. Several of these pamphlets have been issued, and more are coming. Professor Charles Gibson, State University of Iowa, has one on "The

Colonial Period in Latin American History," Professor
Charles G. Sellers, Jr. of Princeton has one on "Jacksonian
Democracy," Professor Otis Singletary of The University of
Texas has one on "The South in American History," Professor Ray Allen Billington of Northwestern University has
an excellent one on "The Westward Movement." Professor
Phil Jordon, University of Minnesota, has one on "The Nature and Practice of Local History." These valuable aids can
be had singly for 50 cents, and in quantity for 10 cents each.
They are written by specialists and intended to help the high
school teacher.

b. A second service is that of providing consultants from
the nearby colleges and universities to attend teachers' meetings, talk to high school students, seek out in the high schools
gifted students, and provide some inducement for them to
go to college.

c. A third service is to give support to such programs as
you have here where teachers are brought together to discuss
their common problems and to be preached at a little by such
as I.

The design, you see, is to bring the professional historian
and the high school teacher together in mutual aid. Certainly,
it is important for you, the history teacher, to know that aid
is available, and that all you need do to get it is to write the
American Historical Association, 400 A Street, S. E., Washington 3, D. C. It is in this way that you can break the isolation in which many of you work, and it is encouraging to
know that a national organization stands ready to assist if
you will call on it.

2. How and Why the Problem We Are
Dealing with Arose

I now come to the second division of my story: How
and why the problem we are dealing with arose. This story
has its humiliating aspects, and the historians themselves—
not the history teachers—bear most of the blame. What I

146

am talking about is, to quote Dr. George Carson, the "growing gap" that has come to exist between the historian, the specialist in the university, and the struggling teacher who is trying to peddle his wares to the reluctant customers in the high schools. Who departed from whom? Did the teachers abandon the historians? Did the historians desert the teacher? Why is the gap a growing gap?

The university professor of history would deny that he deserted the teacher of history, but he will admit that he practically forgot him, ceased to pay much attention to him. He did this, some thirty or forty years ago, because of the nature of a university. In the high school, the function of the historian is to teach; in a university the function of the historian is two-fold, to teach and to do research. In the high school, teaching and teaching only is ordinarily rewarded. In a university teaching is expected, but it is not rewarded to any extent. The thing that brings promotion in rank, increase in salary, admission to the graduate school, and the comforts of an endowed chair is writing, research, production, articles, monographs, books. The history teacher is busy conveying well-known knowledge to those who have little; the university professor is presumably busy discovering new knowledge and conveying it into the realm of things known. In view of this difference in attitude it is not difficult to understand why there is a great deal of good teaching in the high schools and a considerable amount of bad teaching in the universities. Nor is it strange that there is a gap between the historians and the teachers of history.

But why does Dr. Carson speak of a *growing* gap? To explain why the gap is widening, we need to go back about forty years and note the evolution of the university in these western states. Thirty years ago, or maybe forty, the western universities were not universities except in name. They were colleges. They granted the B.A. degree, and an occasional M.A., but the Ph.D. was practically unknown. And in those days the university professors were very close to the high school teachers. The main business of the universities then was to staff the high schools, and the main outlet for the professor's product—the B.A. graduate—was in the high school. The professor kept up with him, visited him occasionally to give a commencement address. The university professor was proud of his student who was doing a good job, and maybe using the professor's textbook.

Then about thirty years ago the colleges that were called universities set out to become universities. They did this by creating the graduate school, and by setting aside the top professors as members of the graduate faculty with a marked increase in pay and a reduction in hours. Every professor of history now wanted to be a graduate professor of history. He wanted to handle graduate students who were fewer in number, less rebellious in nature, and often quite helpful in forwarding his research. He got special credit for the number of M.A.'s and Ph.D.'s he directed, but nothing special for the B.A.'s. The B.A.'s were down graded, came to have the status of a congressman at large, did not belong to anybody. Not so with the M.A.'s; less so with the prize product, the Ph.D.'s. They belonged to the professor and he was most solicitous of them. He helped them get, not high school jobs, but college jobs, and he kept—and keeps—close contact with them.

Not only did the graduate professor forget the high school teacher in order to guide the new Ph.D.'s in their college jobs, but the struggling mass of undergraduate professors also forgot him. The undergraduate professor's purpose now was to climb into graduate work, and this he could do only by producing, writing books, monographs, articles, book reviews, all that dull stuff that clutters up the national meetings and the professional journals. In short all university eyes were turned away from the teacher in the high schools, whether of history or some other subject. Thus the gap continued to grow.

Into this widening gap moved about thirty years ago or

forty a new influence, a new educational philosophy to take over where the professors had left off. The abandonment of the high school teachers by the university professors and the introduction of a radical philosophy of education which swept like a prairie fire over the public school system of the nation explain the educational crisis with which we are now so deeply concerned. I want to speak of this revolution in personal terms because I have seen the whole thing.

When I started to school in Stephens County, in West Texas, more than sixty years ago, it was generally understood by those simple people that the purpose of a school was to teach young folks to read intelligently, write legibly, and make simple arithmetical calculations accurately. It was believed then that those skills would be useful for any who went to college or out into life. The subjects weren't supposed to be easy. They were intended to be difficult and the hours in school were not enough to master them. There was no law then against homework, and you had to do it to get along amicably with McGuffy, Webster, and Ray, and the patron saints of reading, spelling and figuring. If you did well with these taskmasters, you would in time move on to Wentworth, Reed and Kellog and even to Latin and rudimentary science. It was not imperative that you move on, but if you moved you earned the promotion by ability and work. This curriculum contained what was left of the classical tradition of education; it bore a strong resemblance to the trivium and quadrivium of the Renaissance. It had served such men as Washington and Jefferson, Ben Franklin, Webster and Calhoun, men who never dreamed you could learn to read without knowing the alphabet or do problems in mathematics without mastering the multiplication table.

Early in this century this revolution started, bringing a profound change in the purpose and the practice of education. Somebody discovered that the child was more important than the subject, that he was a delicate organism, that the old subjects were harder to master and therefore very bad for the child, and therefore ought to be thrown out. The harder the subject the farther you threw it, first Latin and Greek, then mathematics and any foreign language. The child became the supreme judge of what he ought to learn, and this led to the elective system, and some think to educational chaos. This chaos was called child-centered education.

It was my misfortune to witness the introduction of this new system into my own state. It came to a large south Texas city in 1915 under the guidance of a newly imported superintendent fresh from the fountainhead of the revolutionary philosophy. In this high school the only required subject was English; everything else was elective, but those who expected to go to college were advised to take something besides Navajo rug weaving and telephone post climbing. This superintendent had all the zeal of a new convert as he took the message to Garcia. He kept a large staff compiling figures to show how superior his system was to the old-fashioned schools elsewhere in the state and he spent most of his time lecturing to other superintendents for such fees as could be extracted from their school boards. He was, in the language of James Michener, a Big Dealer.

I hope nobody explains to me later the reasons for this revolution. I know all these reasons and I admit that some of them have merit. But like other revolutions, this one was carried too far by such zealots as my South Texas superintendent.

This revolution started the old classic subjects in retreat, which finally became almost a riot. Latin died out, mathematics became more of a mystery than it was before, and the foreign language teachers saw their classes wither and die. The other courses of substance—such as history, government and literature—became watered down so that these tender children would not be subjected to the slightest intellectual strain. This change came just at a time when we could least afford it.

While this deterioration was going on in the educational

150

field, our civilization was coming to depend more and more on technology on what we were discarding. This technology was largely dependent on chemists and engineers who had no choice but to learn the hard subjects that were dying in the public schools. The colleges and the universities beat a slow retreat, but they had to yield ground too. They either had to teach elementary courses in language, mathematics and science that should have been taught in the high schools, or they had to discard the requirements they had hitherto made. Actually, they did a little of both with the results that standards were gradually lowered at a time when the demand for rigidly trained and educated people was increasing. The revolution had now reached its extreme point and the time of reaction had come. It is here now.

We are here as a part of that reaction. We are here to say whether we want to return to more rigid standards, whether we want our children to learn to work during their youth, whether we want them to discipline their minds or to remain children intellectually until they die of old age. We are here to deal with a crisis in public education—a sort of dry rot—which extends from the elementary grades to the university graduate.

Lest you think I have exaggerated what happened in this revolution, I want to read a description of it, which appeared on the editorial page of the *Wall Street Journal* of April 7, 1958. The author is Mortimer Smith, executive secretary of the Council for Basic Education. The title is "Rx for Education: Not Money Alone but Rigor and Vigor in Class." He begins by saying that we need more than money to build a sound system.

"Even a casual student of the history of education in this country," says Mr. Smith, "must acknowledge that we have been witnessing during the past 40 years nothing less than a revolution in education philosophy—in our conception of the purpose of the schools . . . .

"I think it began with the Deweyean progressives,

151

roughly about 1915, gaining momentum in the 1920's. The early advocates of progressive education have a great deal to answer for, especially on the philosophical side, for theirs was an inadequate view of the nature of man. They lacked a genuine value system, they insisted that the aim in education is simply undefined growth . . . growth and change without much relation to the question: growth towards what? But the . . . educational controversy today is not between progressives and traditionalists; it is between those who believe the school is primarily the agency for the intellectual development of individuals and those who believe it is primarily an agency for social conditioning."

The author concludes that our present trouble is due to the fact that we have been led to accept a pedagogy which "encourages soft testing, soft guidance, soft language and science requirements, soft teacher preparation, and soft curricula generally. We have forgotten what is central in our tender regard for what is peripheral . . .; we have lost sight of the fact that the purpose of schools is to make young people literate in the various fields of organized human knowledge."

Again I come back to the query with which I started, the subject of my remarks: What are we here for? We are here, I think, on behalf of the organized fields of human knowledge which are now being reconsidered as subjects worthy of study, serious study, in the system of public education. I represent history as it is taught in the universities and better colleges, but I have no intention of getting tedious about the value of history and the other social and humanistic subjects. We of the content subjects realize that we can not turn back the tide of soft pedagogy which has already enveloped the nation. We certainly can not expect those who have made the revolution, who have thrown out or reduced or belittled the field of organized knowledge to place them back in the curriculum, and thereby confess that they were wrong in the first place. If the content courses are restored it will be with the knowledge and support of parents, laymen, and teachers.

Actually the reform is already well under way. Beginning about 1950, a great public outcry went up because Johnny couldn't read, Mary couldn't spell, and Billy had trouble determining what two plus two equaled. There wasn't much organization in the first attack which broke out spontaneously in widely scattered places. But some progress was made. The universities and colleges got bold enough to put in entrance examinations and give intelligence tests to shut out the incapable and the totally unfit. The public grumbled a little, then accepted, and is now near to applauding entrance examinations. Word has gone down to the high schools to hold up the hands of the teachers who tried to hold up standards. Languages are being restored in the high schools, and Latin classes are being re-established. The colleges and universities had during the revolution lost touch with the public schools, leaving them in the hands of the revolutionary forces. They, the universities and colleges, are now re-establishing contact, resuming responsibilities which they had all but abandoned. The talented students in the various fields of organized human knowledge are being sought and encouraged to go on to institutions of higher learning just like football players are.

In the colleges and universities the good students are receiving special attention. They are being singled out and sent into honors courses. Study, even a little homework, is becoming respectable, and the teachers with high standards are being supported by administrators and by parents.

It is a mistake to assume that students do not like work, and to work hard. They will accept softness, but they do not necessarily prefer it, and they never respect it. They are in a curriculum, and the first meaning of that word is a running, a racecourse. They like to run, and run hard. Moreover, they recognize fraud when they find it. This was never illustrated better than in a cartoon I saw some years ago. It showed a distraught teacher and a small child in a tantrum, face distorted, fists doubled. The child was shouting to the teacher: "I don't want to express myself. I want to learn to read and write." Then there was the other child, inquiring naively of his progressive teacher: "Do I have to do what I want to?"

The writer I quoted earlier intimated in his article that this lax system of soft education is responsible for the wave of anti-intellectualism which swept over this country during the past two decades. This is a grave charge to bring against any educational system. The charge may not be true, but there is logic in it. There are signs now that anti-intellectualism may be passing away, that the prejudice against the intellectual is declining. It was in the midst of this anti-intellectual movement that a derogatory word was coined to describe the thoughtful person. The word was "egghead." Certain editorial writers loved the term, and used it to damn men whose views they did not like.

Probably *The Saturday Evening Post,* with its 5,750,000 circulation, represents the common denominator in American literary taste and opinion. I suspect that an examination of its files during the past twenty years would reveal that it joined in the chase of the intellectuals, and that it used the derogatory term, "egghead," more than once in its editorials.

Therefore, I could hardly believe my eyes when I picked up the *Post* for April 26, 1958, and found that the *Post* had come over on the side of the intellectual, the thinker. With a blare of the editorial trumpet, the *Post* announced a series of articles entitled "Adventures of the Mind." The articles, the *Post* says, are "written by some of the world's ablest creative thinkers."

The *Post* editors were a little self-conscious about reversing themselves. They justified their act in a page of large type. They warn their 5,750,000 readers that they will have to concentrate to read these men. They believe, they say, that "our audience has enough intellectual curiosity to justify the series."

No country boy ever brought his city bride into the presence of his family on the farm with more trepidation and misgiving than the *Post* editors showed in introducing the intellectuals to the large motley family of *Post* readers. The editors did their best to explain the good points of each to the other, and hope for the best.

> "Perhaps," they said, "never before . . . has the . . . *Post* undertaken so ambitious a project as the one we are launching. . . . We call this new series ADVENTURES OF THE MIND because creative thinking can be high adventure. [Just think of it!]
>
> "For some . . . little time we . . . have been deeply disturbed by the obvious—and obviously dangerous—chasm that separates the intellectuals . . . from the millions of citizens whose attitudes and opinions determine national policy and set the standards of national behavior.
>
> "The intellectual, or 'egghead' (as we carelessly brand him), has deep reservations about the layman. He feels that we don't understand him, or respect him, or reward his labors. . . . And so he goes his cloistered way. . . .
>
> "The rest of us, meanwhile, struggle with more routine problems of an ever more complex world—buffeted by currents that we sense rather than comprehend, mistrustful of the 'egghead' who has never 'met a payroll' or a sales quota.
>
> "The Russian Sputnik . . . produced a gigantic upheaval in American life. It raised questions about our schools, our economy, our self-satisfaction, our moral fiber. Suddenly all of us are required to consider problems of national values and survival that did not seem to exist yesterday. The irony is that these problems . . . are the very problems the intellectuals have been grappling with for decades."

The editors made clear the part the Russians have played in making us aware of the educational crisis we are in. The crisis of soft education was on us before Sputnik circled the earth. What Sputnik did was to frighten us into doing something about the crisis. Maybe it is now becoming clear why we are here and what we are here for. If the bankers, lawyers, executives and directors and the labor leaders want a better educational system, they can have it by demanding it, by building a bridge of communication between themselves and those in the schools and colleges who believe that the purpose of the schools is to make young people literate in the various fields of organized human knowledge. There are still such people.

3. What Has Been Done on the Program in Texas

I now come to the third part of this address which I give only because I was requested to tell you what has been done in my state, which is Texas. In recent years Texas has been the butt of many jokes, most of them of indifferent quality. I mention Texas as little as possible when I am abroad because people seem to be a little tired of hearing about what sort of place it is. This attitude was reflected in the story of the Texan who went to New York and put in a long distance telephone call. He told the operator to report the charge so that he could pay it. When the operator told him the charge was $16 he blew a fuse and started berating the company and the service. He ended his tirade by saying, "Why, in Texas I could phone to hell and back for less than sixteen dollars." The operator who had remained silent up to now, as she is instructed to do, said: "Yes, that is correct, sir, but in Texas it would be a local call."

Since I have always been interested in the teaching of history in the high school, and was brought on to the University because I was considered a pretty successful high school teacher, I accepted an invitation from Dr. Carson to read a paper on the subject at the Chicago meeting of the American Historial Association in 1956. There I told Dr. Carson that if he would give us a part of that $148,000 he had to spend we would be his guinea pig. He gave us $800, and we persuaded Dr. James Taylor of the San Marcos State College to take a leave of absence and make a study of the history teaching problems of the state. Dr. Taylor was especially well qualified to do this because he was one college

156

teacher who had kept in touch with the history teachers of Texas.

We at the University had lost touch completely, and we wanted a survey made that would reacquaint us with the facts, bring us up to date.

Dr. Taylor began work in February and continued his travels until May 3, 1958. In that period he visited twenty school systems, including Houston, Dallas-Fort Worth, and Beaumont where he spent several days because these are very large systems with a great many schools. He spent the $800 in providing speakers and partial expenses, for conferences at four colleges in various parts of the state. (I will say that The University of Texas paid Dr. Taylor's salary and all his traveling expenses. The funds from the Service Center were given to the local committees in these four conferences.)

Professor Taylor learned many things, some of which follow:

Beginning September 1, 1958, the State Board of Education, acting through the Educational Agency will require all high school graduates to take the following:

One unit in world history

One unit in U.S. History

One-half unit in Government

He learned that the teachers are not prepared to teach world history because the universities and few of the colleges offer such courses. If historians are really in earnest about giving some service to the public school teachers, they will get away from their specialties long enough to give a course for teachers in world history.

Professor Taylor learned that many administrators assume no special training is required to teach history and the social studies. He found one school where there were fourteen teachers of social studies, and nine of them were athletic coaches. This criminal practice should be stopped. He did not report any case where the history teacher with no knowledge of football was asked to coach the football team.

In his final report Professor Taylor recommended that the history department employ a competent person to do these things:

1. Give during the long session a course in the teaching of history. This course will be given at the undergraduate level. It would be repeated during the summer.

2. Give a six hour course in World History which would prepare the teachers to teach World History. This course would involve a survey of the entire field. The students would be expected to master a textbook, and in each semester develop two topics in depth. The course would break in the eighteenth century. The topics for intensive study in the first semester would be the Islamic Civilization; and the Protestant Revolution. For the second semester, the topics would be the French Revolution and the World Wars.

We at The University of Texas have acted on Professor Taylor's recommendations. We have employed Professor James Pearson under a three year contract to give these courses, to attend meetings of history and social studies teachers throughout the state, to seek out the star history students and encourage them to continue the work in which they are gifted.

The Texas Education Agency now requires that every high school student take a course in World History. The curriculum as now visualized will offer the social studies on the following schedule:

8th grade—Political and Economic Geography
9th grade—U.S. History (Required)
10th grade—Elective optional in world geography
11th grade—World History (Required)
12th grade—Civics ½ or 1 unit (½ required)

There is another way in which the gap between the history teacher and the university professor can be narrowed. That is for the history teacher to move over from the function of teaching into the realm of writing and research. There is something about writing and the preparation to do it effectively that transforms the individual, makes him a different person. As long as you confine your effort to teaching, you reach only those who come within the sound of your voice. When you write something, and find a publisher for it, you extend your ideas to a vast and unseen audience; you communicate to all sorts of people. If what you write is good, you receive letters of commendation and blame. The preparation to write and the ordeal of writing sharpens your perception and makes you aware of more things to write about. The real writer is never at a loss for subjects. They literally jump out of the bushes at him on every side. If your writing has merit, it leads to new contacts, to new jobs, to promotion into the colleges and universities, if that means anything.

When you write, publish, and don't be choosy about the place in which you publish. If you can't start with the national magazines, then start with the local magazines or the local paper. Publish anywhere.

The public schools are filled with people, some of whom want to write. There are many who can write, and yet rarely do. I am thinking of a little woman who teaches the third grade. She wrote an M.A. thesis with me on a pretty tough subject. I saw that she had a natural talent for writing, and so I began to question her.

"Have you done any writing?" I asked.

"No, don't have time."

"Why don't you have time?"

"I have to paint the fence."

"Well, you might write something that would enable you to have somebody else paint the fence."

"What would I write about?"

"About your adventures in the classroom, as a teacher."

She had been telling the most excruciatingly funny stories about these kids, the absurd things they said and did, the jams they got her into.

"If I wrote about what goes on in my classroom," she said, "I'd get fired."

159

"We'll get you a better job," I said.

She went back to her school for a year, and returned the next summer with those beautiful chapters which were really too good for an M.A. thesis.

"Did you do anything on that writing?" I asked.

"No. Didn't have time." Then she told me.

"I did gather a box of notes, things said and done in class. Yes, and one night I couldn't go to sleep, and I thought of a title for the book. I also thought of some chapter headings."

"What is your title?" I asked.

"Thirty Years in the Third Grade."

The title is a natural. Anybody who ever taught school would be intrigued by that title, and would open the book to find humor, pathos, wit, and all the qualities that make for delightful reading.

When I had recovered from the shock of this title, I asked, "What are some of your chapter headings?"

She gave two pregnant with humor. The first, "Papa's On the School Board"; second, "Hi-o, maderio, the P.T.A."

She completed her thesis, returned to her third graders, and I have heard no more from her. The mystery to me is why anyone with such insight and such talent for words does not do something about it.

There may not be many people like her, but there are many talented people in the public schools who could do much to close the gap between them and the university professors. Power to them.

XIII LEARNING and WISDOM:
the RELEVANCE of HISTORY

J MUST admit that I was very much pleased when Dr. Herbert Gambrell asked me to participate in the celebration of the fiftieth anniversary of the founding of Southern Methodist University. This university is especially dear to me because it gave me a degree without requiring anything in return, and there is nothing that an alumnus enjoys more than to be requested to do something —almost anything—for his alma mater.

I must confess that I was a little startled at the prescription laid down by Dr. Gambrell for this performance. He stated that this part of the program was to be a seminar, that it was to begin at 2:30 and end by 6 o'clock. I have become accustomed to seminars that run from four and one-half to nine months, and it had never occurred to me that one could be completed in such a short time. Thinks I, this seminar must be on a small subject. But Dr. Gambrell blithely stated that the general subject was to be "Learning and Wisdom" and that this seminar would pertain to "The Relevance of History." I suppose he means the relevance of history to learning and wisdom. If this is the sort of assignment Dr. Gambrell hands out to his students, then I am indeed glad that S.M.U. gave me a degree rather than run the risk of my earning it under his supervision. I have never seen a program packed with more assumptions:

1. That a seminar could be completed in three and one-half hours.

2. That anyone knows anything about the relationship between learning and wisdom, where one leaves off and the other begins.

3. That anyone knows the relevance of history to learning, and especially to wisdom.

4. The final, and most brazen assumption is that I am qualified to say anything worthwhile on this subject. But here I am compelled to say something, and here you are compelled to listen.

It seems a little strange that Dr. Gambrell would do this to us. All of you know that he is a modest and retiring person, shy almost to a fault. He would himself shrink from doing what he has required of us and that is to talk out of our experiences about learning, wisdom, and the relevance of history. He wants us to reveal our ego which he will never do himself. He has forgotten, or ignored, what the Lord Chesterfield told his son when he was trying to make a gentleman of him. "Two things you should never exhibit in public," Lord Chesterfield said, "and that is your watch and your learning." He never heard until now what I heard a country philosopher say when I was a boy in West Texas. "There are two things if you've got you don't need to talk about; one is money and the other is brains." The only thing Dr. Gambrell has not required us to exhibit or talk about is our money.

All that I have said is preliminary to what I shall exhibit

soon. While I may not like it, I want to make it clear that I am aware of what I am doing. The only thing I can do is to speak out of my own experience of the relevance of history, perhaps with some implications as to learning and wisdom.

I have written two books in which I take considerable pride, *The Great Plains* and *The Great Frontier*. They are alike in two respects. Each deals with the frontier and each is based on a thesis or hypothesis. Whatever claim I may eventually have to either learning or wisdom must be based on these two books. The other books I have written will not be notable for either. Rather than use the terms thesis and hypothesis, I would prefer the term, idea, and say that each book is based on a single idea.

The idea behind *The Great Plains* is a very simple one, so simple that no one had seen it before, or more correctly I should say that no one developed and illustrated it. The idea was that continental United States consists of two great environments separated approximately by the 98th meridian which almost exactly bisects the nation. East of this center line lies the Great Eastern Woodland, broken in topography, heavily timbered, and humid in climate. West of this central line lies the Great Plains region, level, treeless and semi-arid or arid in climate. The American pioneers spent about two and one-half centuries in the Eastern Woodland, and in that time worked out a technique of living adapted to a humid, forested and rolling land. About the middle of the nineteenth century or a little before, they emerged from the forest and entered the open plain where the conditions of living were reversed. There was no timber and never enough water, and as a result, the thesis contends, their whole system of pioneering broke down, and the techniques they had used so successfully would no longer work. In a gigantic experiment carried on by thousands, the pioneers modified their ideas, practices and techniques to serve the new environment. Once the idea of looking for what happened when civilization came out of the woods and undertook to live in a level, treeless, semi-arid land was clear, the procedure was plain and the task simple. It was to inquire as to what changes took place in weapons, in fencing, in procuring water, in plows and in methods of farming, and in laws pertaining to land and to water. The 98th meridian was established as an institutional fault line and practically every institution that was carried across that line was bent or modified.

This central idea was so simple that once I had it, I marveled that no one else had exploited it. During the time that the book was in preparation, I hesitated to open any new book on the American West for fear something so clear to me had been seen by another. A friend of mine, commenting on it, summed my situation up by saying that "Webb's talent consists in making people conscious of the obvious." I think this dubious compliment is true, so far as *The Great Plains* is concerned.

Many people are curious as to how an idea around which a book is written originates. I don't think you find an idea such as this by looking for it. When you begin to look for it, you have already found it. It comes to you unawares, and like Carl Sandburg's fog, on little cat feet. It comes to you when you are looking for something else, and suddenly there it is. It is a case of serendipity, once defined as a combination of serenity and stupidity. It comes after you have already acquired a great many facts surrounding it and illustrating it, but not until the unifying idea does come are you aware of the meaning and the significance of the facts. Once it comes the facts fall into ranks and form patterns of meaning. The French historian, Fustel Coulanges, stated it best when he said, "Years of research for one moment of synthesis." It may be called intuitive insight.

I have a most vivid recollection of when the idea around which the *The Great Plains* was written came to me. It was a stormy night when the winter rain beat hard on the roof of a back room where I was working on an article for a magazine put out by a crooked oil company in Fort Worth. It

164

must have been in 1920 or 1921 when the oil boom in West Texas had about reached its peak. At the time I was engaged in writing the history of the Texas Rangers who had been very busy running the outlaws out of the boom towns, such as Ranger, Desdemona, Mexia. This crooked oil company wrote to the University asking that someone do a series of articles for *The Owenwood Magazine.* The letter found its way to my desk and I agreed to do the articles for two cents a word. By way of preparation I was reading Emerson Hough's little book, *The Way to the West.* Hough stated four instruments that were used in the conquest of the frontier: the horse, the boat, the axe and the rifle.

In studying the Texas Rangers I had become familiar with their affinity, not to say affection, for the six-shooter. I asked myself a question: Why did Hough not mention the six-shooter as a fifth instrument in this conquest? I suppose I had a good deal of learning about the Rangers. I knew that they fought Indians, Comanches mainly, and that these Indians came on horseback from the treeless land to the west. Suddenly I saw that the six-shooter was the ideal weapon for a mounted man, better than the rifle, far better than the sword or lance. It was then, there, that night, that I saw the significance of the dividing line between the timberland and the open plain. There I had my moment of synthesis, that I experienced the thrill of serendipity, of looking for one thing and finding something else of far more importance. I knew in an instant that night what it took me a year to prove. I remember the trouble I had in finding out where the timber left off and the plain began. I wrote the story of the six-shooter which was published in *Scribner's Magazine.*

I felt that there was more in the subject than a change in weapons, that some other changes must have taken place when American civilization came out of the woods to live on the plains. A chance remark by E. E. Davis that the settlement of West Texas was made possible by windmills and barbed wire supplied the clue. When I got the facts I found that when men came out of the woods and had no rails they invented barbed wire, and that when they came from the humid country into an arid one they had to find new ways of obtaining water, using the cheapest commodity of the plains, the wind. I now had three stakes lined up in a row, leading west. The rest was easy, though it required a lot of work which may be classed as learning. The pieces fitted together and formed a pattern, from the physical geography at the base of the literature at the crown of the edifice.

Here I might speak briefly of the power of an idea to galvanize a lazy man and set him to work. This idea I had discovered was overpowering, and no obstacle was great enough to divert me from its pursuit. I had to learn some geology, botany, zoology, anthropology, law, literature and of course some history. I read or examined a ton of books, and became so magnetized for what I needed that anything pertaining to the Great Plains seemed to jump out of the page at me. I have never worked with a greater sense of exaltation. After long hours I would be completely exhausted, but the next morning I would return to the subject as a man to his mistress. After eight years of study I wrote the book in about five months. I forgot to say that I threw the Texas Rangers aside until it was finished.

The Great Frontier was published twenty-one years later. The idea for it came one spring morning about 1936 when I was writing another book, *Divided We Stand*. The experience was not nearly as dramatic as in the previous case, but it was exciting. It, too, is written around a single idea, not different in character from that in the Great Plains. The line this time was drawn between the Metropolis of Western Europe and all the new ends discovered by Columbus and his associates around 1500, which I called the Great Frontier. Here again I was concerned with people in transition, the people of Western Europe moving out into the new country. The emphasis was not so much on what these migrating people did to the new country, but what the raw frontier did to them, and to

166

those they left behind. The primary thesis is that the acquisition of so much new land, so many new resources by the poverty-stricken nations of Western Europe upset all the old relations between man and land, between man and the precious metals which flowed in such quantities from the frontier to the Metropolis, between man and wealth. The economic effect was to precipitate a boom on Western Civilization, a boom that lasted about four hundred years, until the frontier in all the new continents had closed. If this be true, and it is almost as obvious as the things pointed out in *The Great Plains,* then the civilization we call modern came into being and grew to maturity during a boom. They are in a real sense boom institutions, adapted to serve the needs of a booming society. The two institutions which flourished and matured during this are modern democracy and modern capitalism. It is possible that the future historians, filled with learning and wisdom, will view the series of wars and revolutions we have known since 1914 as an effort of the nations to adjust to a frontierless world. It is pretty obvious that since 1914 democracy has been under attack, since 1917 modern capitalism has been on the defensive, and both have been in slow retreat. The individual, who was the spoiled darling of the frontier, now that his patrimony is gone, finds himself wedged in and seems to be losing his identity to the corporations on the one hand and to stricter government controls and domination on the other.

It is obvious that a study which reaches such conclusions will not meet with universal acceptance. People—many of them—are unwilling to believe that something precious which they had for four hundred years, something that showered down on them the wherewithal of wealth, liberty and adventure, and unexampled opportunity for a personal achievement is gone forever. They eagerly hunt for a new frontier and are frustrated because they cannot find it. Some are willing to believe that science will bring it back. Recently a ghost writer put the term New Frontier in the mouth of an attractive and unusually intelligent young politician, and he used it most effectively as an emotional device in the campaign that made him President. He has as yet not told us the exact nature of this new frontier, and I doubt that he ever will. Neither science nor politics can in this modern crowded world give us a frontier comparable in any sense to the one we have lost. All that either can do is to manipulate and re-arrange what we have. Neither can offer us on this earth the roominess of two or three new and untarnished continents.

Let us return for a moment to learning, wisdom and the relevance of history. In pursuit of the ideas developed in these two studies, I myself learned a great deal and in com-pelling my graduate students in seminars to hunt in through the wilderness of books in the libraries I compelled them to learn something. As a matter of fact, if I may paraphrase Henry Adams, they dug holes all over the Great Plains and the Great Frontier and brought what they found in to me and their companions. I think I can say that an idea, once it is made clear, can act as a powerful stimulus to a student in that it enables him to know what he is looking for. A few of these students, but not many, are still hunting.

Elton Miles of Sul Ross College became interested in the effect the Great Frontier had on modern literature, and par-ticularly on the romantic literature. It is possible, and I think quite probable, that Miles will write a book that will have a revolutionary effect on literary interpretation. I quote from his letter of April 6.

> (When in Austin) I came by to see you but did not find you in. Then I went to the library where I was able to confirm what I had suspected, that the romantic idea that man is more basically good than bad, as it got its start in the 17th century, is associated with the American noble savage. I find this in Shaftesbury, the Englishman from whom Rousseau and others got some of their best ideas. It scares me sometimes when I make up my mind that something "must be" true and then find objective evidence that it is.

168

As to wisdom, it like the wind, "bloweth where it listeth, and thou . . . canst not tell whence it cometh, and whither it goeth." Wisdom is a chancy thing and any man would be a fool to claim that he has it. Time and posterity determine this issue, and their opinion is usually rendered posthumously. If the findings and the conclusions in the books I have discussed are sustained over a long period of time, if the ideas presented enter into the fabric of thought and become a part of the cloth of history, then the few people who take the trouble to learn where the ideas originated may decide that the historian had some wisdom. Actually, I do not recall having read anywhere that any historian had wisdom, learning, yes, but not wisdom. That term seems to be reserved for philosophers, mystics, and maybe poets.

If Dr. Gambrell had been less philosophic, mystic and poetic in his assignment, he might have asked us to discuss the relevance of history to life. I have tried to make what I have written relevant to it. I have never made any conscious effort to be learned, or to exhibit learning. I have never written for the scholars, but always for the people. I have attempted to make clear to the people the nature of the problems they and their ancestors faced on the Great Plains and on the Great Frontier and to explain how and why they succeeded or failed in their attempts to solve them. I think I can say now that I had some luck with the Great Plains because I made them conscious of the obvious. The task was more difficult with the Great Frontier because the canvas was bigger, the experience more remote, and the situation far more complicated. If what I have written as history is not relevant to life itself it is not relevant to learning and has not the slightest connection with wisdom. It is not even history.

XIV   HYPOTHESIS and HISTORY

WEBSTER tells us that an hypothesis is: "A proposition, condition, or principle which is assumed, perhaps without belief, in order to draw out its logical consequences and by this method to test its accord with facts which are known or may be determined."

I would say that an hypothesis is an intuition or something which may turn out through investigation to be either true or false. If the facts gathered after it appears do not sustain it, the scholar discards it and no more is heard of it. If the facts do sustain it, or if the scholar thinks they do, he develops it and finally he may announce it through publication or through his teaching. Once he announces it, places it in the public domain, other scholars seize upon it, test it, and often seek to destroy it. Those who are convinced by it may develop the details and support it. If it survives both its friends and its foes, if it lives, it does so because it has proved valid for at least a number of those who consider it. By this time the idea has moved out of the hypothesis stage and becomes a theory, bearing the name usually of its originator, such as Newton in Physics, Hutton in Geology, Darwin in Biology, Einstein in Physics, Sumner in Sociology, Adam Smith and John Maynard Keynes in Economics, Spengler, Pareto, Turner and Toynbee in History. All these men are famous, and a great burden to undergraduates, because each in his own way hit upon an hypothesis which turned out to have some validity. Five of them, three in science, one in economics, and one in sociology are spoken of with great respect as fathers of a discipline. You will note that no historian has ever become father of a discipline. The best a historian has been able to do is to beget a school, which is a considerable cut below a discipline. The reason for this intellectual inadequacy, though not complete sterility, I will attempt to explain later.

The examples given above, and a hundred others could be added, illustrate that the hypothesis is widely used by scholars and thinkers in many fields. It may not be used by scholars, but it is the universal instrument of the thinker. The scholar may become recognized as such by digging up facts, and he need not even classify them. But once he begins to seek the meaning of the facts, he has to start the process of thinking, and when he does this he is likely to come up with an hypothesis as to what the facts mean.

If the above analysis is correct, then we are in a position to make some observations as to where the individual is in his career when the hypothesis arrives. It is doubtful if any man ever set out to hunt the hypothesis that made him his reputation. Had he done this he would have had his hypothesis already, and he would not need to hunt for it. But no man ever found an important hypothesis who had not *set out,* who was not already an investigator, an observer, an industrious gatherer of the facts. His knowledge of the facts, and what others had done with them, would qualify him as a scholar though not necessarily as a thinker. But even though he knew everything in the encyclopedia, was a Teddy Nadler, he would not say to himself some morning, "Now that I know everything, I will seek to announce a world-shaking hypothesis that will make me the father of something." The hypothesis does not come in that way. It is not designed, nor is it consciously sought.

Some bright morning, or more likely in the still hours of the night, it appears, usually, I suspect, when the student-scholar is looking for something else. And there it is, clothed in magic, a vision of truth never perceived so clearly by any other man. To the beholder it is not a hypothesis—it is a truth entrusted to him and he hopes to no other. It is a moment of creation, attended with a feeling of exaltation that is indescribable. It is what he has been waiting for without knowing what he was waiting for, but now that he has it he recognizes it as what he has long wanted. The pleasure of the moment is so intense as to amount to pain.

When this hypothesis arrives it begins to put the intellectual house in order. The numerous facts hitherto so painfully gathered begin moving to form patterns around the central idea. They take on meaning, become a part of the whole. Complex things become simple; confusion almost disappears. The French historian who said: "Years of research for one moment of synthesis."

What astounds the scholar is the simplicity of what he beholds in that moment of synthesis. Why, he says, this is perfectly obvious. Everybody must have seen this. And away he goes to the library to find out. There, if he is fortunate, he will learn that many have seen parts, but none has seen the whole.

It is quite remarkable what a gift people have for overlooking the obvious, for not seeing things whole, and for over-organizing the parts. The great hypotheses that have shaped the intellectual world of thought are, so far as I am able to determine, extremely simple. Newton saw the apple fall. He said the apple and the earth attract each other, and

172

the attraction is relative to the weight of each. Since the apple weighs so much less than the earth it falls to the earth instead of the earth to the apple. And there he had the law of gravitation. Darwin noted that no two individuals are identical, and he called this variation. Some of these diverse individuals are better equipped than others to survive, and he called this the survival of the fittest. And there was the principle of evolution. Two sentences state each of the two more important hypotheses launched in the last 500 years. Two sentences will state most any hypothesis that turns out to be valid, provided the sentences are written by one who understands the hypothesis.

The hypothesis is a highly individual thing. It is not shared with anybody, and in this sense it is like a poem, a painting, or a baby. It has never appeared or been discovered by a committee; and in my opinion, it is not present at conventions. That is something that ought not to be lost sight of in this day of gang scholarship, or, if you prefer a euphemism, directed research. These gangs of scholars may work out details and make the practical application, but the basic idea comes from one man. And more often than not, I suspect, he is something of an idler, or seems to be. He is not full of busyness. Maybe this is what a visitor to a college campus meant when, after he had been there several days, was asked by his host what he thought of the place. "Well," he said, "I do not see enough men sitting in their offices with their feet on the desk looking out the window."

But now I must speak briefly of the effect the hypothesis has on the discoverer. The effect may be summed up by saying it transforms him. It transforms him because it gives him a purpose, and a direction. At last he knows where he is going, and why. He reminds us of the jingle about the little eohippus, the dog-like progenitor of the now highly specialized horse.

> Said the little eohippus, "I'm going to be a horse
> And on my middle fingernail, I'll run my earthly course."

173

In his effort to become a horse the scholar does things that surprise him, develops power he did not know he had, reads books by the ton, magnetizes himself so that the material he needs seems to fly out of the books to him, plumbs subconscious depths he never before touched. And he may be doing his best work when he is sitting with his feet on the desk looking out the window. Even among his fellows, he is living in a world of his own, a world more real to him than what is around him. The world is likely to say that he is eccentric, that he has no common sense, and in this the world is correct, for the kind of sense he has at this stage is most uncommon.

You will note that in discussing the man with the hypothesis I have drawn mostly from the scientists, and said little about the historians. My reason for doing this is that I wanted to clothe the man with the hypothesis with respectability, and of course today science has top billing in respectability, in fact it has become slightly sacred. But for once the scientists are on my side because every one of them who is more than a piece worker in gang research will tell you that the creative scientist works by hypothesis.

The scientist has a great advantage over the humanitarian, the historian for example, because he can prove the truth or the falsity of his theory. He can do this because he is dealing primarily with fixed factors which will repeat their performance for him in the same way whenever he brings them together under the same conditions. If he gets this reaction a thousand times, with no exceptions, he draws up his law and proclaims it to the world. The only reason Newton's law of gravitation is accepted as universal is that no one has yet seen the earth fall to the apple. Actually to the historian who is dealing with a problem where all the factors are variables, and their combination at any moment is unique, the task of the scientist, once he has an idea, seems to be suited to simpletons. Scientists run no risk in the pursuit of hypotheses. They glory in what they prove and bury the rest.

174

The historian has such poor luck with hypotheses that he shuns them. And no wonder. No historian that I know of has ever been able to prove one. Since Herodotus started the racket, no historian has ever drawn up a law of history that had any acceptance. There is none bearing the name of a Kepler or Faraday, not to mention a Newton or Darwin or Einstein. No historian has ever derived a formula, such as $E = MC^2$, that can be applied over and over to human action.

This means that the historical hypothesis never gets beyond the hypothetical stage. It is always controversial, never universal, and the best the historian can hope to get is a split decision. In time, or at times, all historical hypotheses are buried, though the better ones will be resurrected occasionally. Why will the historian engage in a game where the result is always fatal? Most of them refuse to be so foolish. They stick to their facts, record events, write biographies or tell stories that interest them. Some of them mistakenly delude themselves into believing that they are being scientific, and objective. If they are thin-skinned, they avoid the controversy involved in any historical hypothesis. They are perfectionists who want to get something so right that no one can find any fault with it. They prefer to inform the mind rather than to inflame the intellect.

All this is their right and no one should criticize them for exercising it. But many of them go a step farther and develop a philosophy which not only justifies them, but is extremely critical of those who do not do just as they do. They approach any hypothesis with great suspicion which may border on prejudice. They want none of it. And again they are within their right, but there may be one side-effect of this attitude that is regrettable. It is possible that these historians inculcate into their students an excess timidity, make them too conscious of the hazards of criticism, more anxious to avoid a small error than to be caught with a particle of truth. A university, and especially a graduate school, ought to be a place where people take calculated risks, a place of constant adven-

175

ture with enough danger to spice it.

I repeat, in view of all the hazards of the historical hypothesis, why would any historian risk one? Why not stick to the certitudes? The answer to this question is locked up with the other mysteries of the human mind. I think as good an answer as any was given by one of the two young Englishmen, the first human beings to scale Mount Everest.

"Why do men climb mountains?" he was asked.

"Because," he answered, "the mountain is there."

Someday, without his bidding, the hypothesis is there, towering as high as any mountain. He did not make it come, and he cannot make it go away. He wants to see what is on top of it, and so he sets out without counting the risk to see. He climbs it because otherwise he can have no rest, driven as he is by the insatiable curiosity of the investigator. I think that answer might be accepted by all the historical hypothesis climbers.

Up to now I have dealt with the hypothesis in the abstract, in general. From here on I will be more specific and speak, with becoming academic modesty, I trust, of my own limited experience with hypotheses. I have embraced two major hypotheses, and if my name survives after the flag on the esplanade has flown at half mast for me for a half day, it will be because I did so. But I was not in search of immortality, either when I embraced them or as I pursued them. The hypothesis was there. Now I will give you some of my reasons for pursuing it.

1. The pursuit of an hypothesis is a lot of fun. Its first appearance is attended with intense excitement, and its pursuit with unflagging interest. If it develops, it gives one a sensation, whether real or imagined, of creativeness. It gives zest to an otherwise dull life.

2. A second reason, or rather an explanation of why I was fortunate in finding an hypothesis, is not at all to my credit. I am by nature extremely lazy. I inherited, or acquired before I can remember, a strong disinclination to work.

Drudgery never appealed to me, and it doesn't now. Had I not found an hypothesis I probably would have spent my entire academic life looking out windows, dreading to read examination papers, and musing about the prejudice of an administration that would not promote me, and the injustice of things in general. I might even have played a little golf as a relief from my uninterrupted leisure, or made a garden. My hypothesis saved me from doing most of these things. I cannot say that interest in what I was doing cured me of laziness, not at all, but it absorbed me to such an extent that I did not notice it. I actually did an enormous amount of pure drudgery. An hypothesis can really stir you up. I am reminded here of an experience I had with my first automobile, a T Model Ford of four cylinders. I did not know anything about a car, and I could never get that Ford to run right. It would sputter, backfire, hit on three cylinders, do everything but work. The guarantee was still good, and I took it back each day to the Ford mechanic and he would tinker a little and send me away. Finally, he lost patience and said, "Don't bring this car back. There's nothing wrong with it."

"But it doesn't run right," I said. "It misses."

"Well, O.K. The damn thing ain't supposed to run until it gets hot." And so, after much sputter and backfire, I got hot. I wrote *The Great Plains* defending my first hypothesis in four and one-half months.

3. The hypothesis was good for me for a third reason. I am not only lazy, but I have a poor memory, especially for isolated facts. Since they are all in the reference books, to which I have access, I see no reason for memorizing them, even if I could. I proceed by association, by tying things together into a system or pattern. The hypothesis begins with a central idea, and you are always building around that idea, connecting more and more facts and phenomena to it. You always have a place to take off from, and a place to come back to. The central idea, the thesis, in the Great Plains study, was that the western half of this country is so different physically

177

from the eastern half, the plains are so different from the woodland, that when civilization crossed this line from one to the other, the old technique of pioneering broke down, and an entirely new technique had to be evolved. Once equipped with that hypothesis, the process of following the institutions, tools, weapons, even the law across that line and observing the change was almost as simple as the procedure of the scientist. I no longer had to memorize because I knew where the facts belonged, and I could recall them by association. The facts I needed were all related, and in toto form a unified whole.

This matter of relationship is a fourth advantage ensuing from what I would call a major hypothesis. And I will illustrate this advantage by alluding to *The Great Frontier*. The thesis of the Great Frontier study, while gigantic in scope, is extremely simple in principle and can be stated in two sentences. It holds that when Columbus and his associates uncovered three and one-half new continents and laid this Great Frontier in all its freshness in the lap of an impoverished Europe, it upset all the relations that had existed between man and land, between man and the precious metals, between man and wealth or the stuff wealth is made of. The people of the Metropolis began to move out to the Great Frontier and the wealth from the Great Frontier began to flow back on Europe with the result that a boom was precipitated on western civilization which endured as long as the frontier was open, for a period of 400 years. It was in this boom, an abnormal condition, that modern civilization developed, that the idea of progress became current, that our most cherished institutions, notably democracy and capitalism, were born.

I call your attention to the simplicity of the concept. Europe was treated as a unity, without regard to its subdivision into nations, on the one hand, and the Great Frontier, a raw and primitive land, was treated as a unit without regard to its division into continents. Then the drama of modern his-

178

tory consisted of the interaction between these two factors, one bringing civilization to the frontier and the other pouring wealth into the metropolis. Most historians have been historians of civilization, bent on explaining what the metropolis did to the frontier; but since I was frontier-based, I gave most attention to what the frontier did to civilization. They showed how the metropolis made the frontier civilized; I showed how and why the frontier made western civilization rich, enabled it, as John Maynard Keynes said, to afford Shakespeare and culture.

With this simple concept of two gigantic factors interacting on each other, a great many seemingly unrelated things fell into place. And here we come upon one of the most exciting features of a major hypothesis. The major hypothesis may come alone and it usually does. But it is followed soon by a whole progeny of little ones. Out of the metropolis and out of the frontier they clamber for attention.

Time permits me to cite only one example. This minor hypothesis I have called the vertical pulsation of wealth. This subthesis holds that wealth, instead of having one motion, the horizontal motion that the economists teach about, and call circulation, has in modern times had two motions, one horizontal among the members of the society, and the other vertical between the sovereign and the members of the society. If wealth has in modern times really had two motions, and if its action has been explained in terms of one motion, then it would seem that those who have made this explanation may find it necessary to do some more explaining. At any rate here is the way the argument in favor of the dual circulation of wealth goes.

When the Great Frontier was discovered, all these continents and islands became the property of the sovereigns of Europe. Since the sovereigns could not themselves make use of so much land, they began to distribute it to their subjects. That is to say the land sifted down vertically from the man at the top, the sovereign, to the men below. And in every case two things happened: first, the land tended to break up into smaller and smaller units until it got down to just what an individual family could use; second, eventually, if not sooner, this distribution came to be made without cost to the recipient, as a free homestead or as a royal grant. This free dispersion of land to people got under way almost immediately after the discovery of the Great Frontier and it continued at an ever accelerating rate until there was no more frontier; i.e., until about 1900. It was by means of this gigantic land deal that the western sovereigns could cure depressions and level out the economy without taking anything away from anybody. The sovereign simply cut up some more of the Great Frontier and gave it away. When the last depression hit, that of 1930, the sovereign had no more land to give, and his only recourse was to take from some in order to give to others. Had the sovereign power of this country, the government, taken back the western half of America and redistributed it after 1930, this process would have been clear. Instead, today the sovereign takes money up to Washington and recirculates it, so that we have now as a permanent policy the vertical *circulation* of wealth, not only here but throughout western civilization. This is not a new policy, but a new device adopted by the sovereign to enable him to continue a very old policy. Once these simple and indisputable facts are recognized, a great deal of our economic and political history appears in a new light. We may be disturbed, for example, to see that both democracy and modern capitalism flourished best during the centuries when the sovereigns were subsidizing everybody from the bounty of the Great Frontier.

In conclusion I may tell you what happens to him who launches an historical hypothesis. He is lucky if he ends up just a little short of oblivion. The scientist achieves a permanent niche in the hall of fame because he proves his hypothesis. The historian can never prove his, and so there can be no historical hall of fame. Each generation of historians tells his story to his own generation, and then yields his place to an-

180

other who tells a different story to a new generation. The hypothesis is always under attack, as witness Turner, Toynbee, Spengler, and Pareto, to mention some contemporaries. The critics are nibbling away at all of them. In time they will no longer be considered, but if the hypothesis had any real merit, its essence, its central idea may survive. It will be found in a thousand books, become a tiny part of the wisdom of the race, a fleck in the great fabric of history, but few will notice it and scarcely one will know whence it came.

XV The GREAT FRONTIER: an INTERPRETATION

ERHAPS I should explain why I am here. I think
I am here because in teaching such students as I
see, I hit upon an idea about history that I had not
heard from other historians. I thought that this idea of mine
explained much history better than other explanations I
had seen.

Now, when one hits on such an idea—one that explains
things—he begins to interpret, say, what the facts mean in
terms of that idea; he presents a thesis or an interpretation.
It seems all right for a scientist to present a thesis, better
known to him as an hypothesis. He can do this because he
can prove his thesis by observation and experiment and if he
makes it stand up, we attach his name to a law such as
Galileo's Law, Faraday's Law of Physics, and Darwin's
Principle of Evolution.

There is no law bearing the name of any historian. The

reason is that the historian can never prove his hypothesis. He cannot use experiment or make firsthand observation. He can never do the job so well as to have it universally accepted by all historians. If he does interpret history, he is sure to receive criticism and it seems that the more revealing his interpretation is, the more severe the criticism is likely to be.

Though I knew all this, I have ventured two interpretations in history. One was set forth in the first book I wrote, *The Great Plains,* and the other in a later one, *The Great Frontier.* I will define the Great Frontier, state the hypothesis or thesis I have developed about it, and support it with illustrations from modern history. I shall do this boldly, partly because of the time limitation but partly because he who launches a thesis in history catches hell anyway and cannot escape by being timid.

The Great Frontier consists of all the new lands discovered by Columbus and his associates around 1500. It is a century older than the American Frontier that Professor Turner examined and many times larger, comprising three continents and more than half of a fourth, and thousands of islands in the then-unexplored seas. That is the area that I have designated the Great Frontier. Now set over against this vast area, these three and a half continents, the wage of land we know as Europe, the homeland; to this region I have given the name of Metropolis, including in it all of the states, divisions, and nations. This thesis is that the interaction between the civilized metropolis of Europe and the uncultured Great Frontier exerted a profound influence on the drama of Western civilization for more than 450 years and has largely determined the nature of that drama.

For clarity, let me represent the Metropolis and the Great Frontier as the leading characters in a long play, the Metropolis in the feminine role and the Great Frontier in the masculine. As happens often in more personal relations, the lady has much the better of it in culture and refinement and religion and all the arts. But in the economic realm, she is a little down at the heel, with threadbare garments and hardly enough food. Her involuntary reducing diet had been carried to extremes—she has known thirteen famines per century for a very long time. Now from the opposite wing of the stage, we imagine appearing the rude figure of the Great Frontier, with hardly any garments, scarcely any art, no alphabet, little wine, and no whiskey at all. This giant figure, robust and strong, is in possession of material resources of such magnitude as the delicate lady who faces him never dreamed of. Of land he has more than three continents, some forty million quarter-section homesteads, of which in the opinion of the lady he is making poor use.

It is not surprising that these contrasting characters became interested in each other. Each had what the other was out of. The Metropolis had the culture, the Great Frontier had the wealth of the stuff it was made of, more gold than had been mined in all history, more land than could be surveyed in three centuries, grass never cropped by domestic animals, forests never cut by an ax, minerals that had never known a miner. After the union, the Metropolis began to acquire the wealth, and the Great Frontier began to absorb the culture, and in this exchange both were modified, each drew nearer to what the other was, but even now there were differences. The upshot of the alliance was the conversion of a medieval society into a modern one, the evolution of a new set of institutions which we now call modern and which we mistakenly, no doubt, consider permanent. So much for the main thesis.

Once I perceived the frontier hypothesis, much history began to appear in a new perspective. Many subtheses showed up to harmonize with the major thesis and the most important subthesis I have called the Boom Hypothesis of modern history. It holds that our civilization in modern times has existed in a boom. I hold that the sudden injection of three and a half new continents into the economy of Europe made that economy remarkably dynamic as Europeans set off to explore, develop, and exploit the vast new country. As the boom followed, it was possible, and in an acquisitive society such as Europe had, it was almost inevitable. It came primarily because the old and stabilized ratio of population to land, population to the gold and silver, to resources of every description, was upset. It is this ratio of population to land, said William Graham Sumner, which determines what are the possibilities of human development, or the limits of what man can attain in civilization and comfort.

Now let us look at this upset ratio in two categories, in land and in the precious metals. Prior to the opening of the Great Frontier, there were more than 26 people on each square mile in Europe. After the discoveries, there were less than five persons to the square mile in the expanded area. Where before, each person had an average of about 24 acres, each now had about 148 acres or a six-fold increase. The exploitation of this land sent wave after wave of wealth pouring back on the Metropolis. The first wave and one of the most spectacular was the gold and silver that the Spaniards found when they cracked the treasure houses of the New World. In 1500, Europe had a population of about 100 million and it had about $200 million, all told. In other words, each person had two dollars. By 1600, a century later, the population had not increased appreciably, but the gold and silver had jumped sixfold giving each individual twelve dollars instead of two. By 1700, the population had increased 25 per cent. The gold and silver had increased nearly eighty times the rate of the population increase. The boom, you see, stood on three legs: an excess of land, an excess of gold and silver, and an excess of goods and commodities in relation to the number of people to provide them. This situation proved to be temporary because the population was the variable factor and began to rise and to fill up the land, and that rise is constantly accelerated.

By 1930, the year of the world depression, the population per square mile in the Western world passed the population in the Metropolis in 1500. One leg supporting the boom, the excess of land, had collapsed, and henceforth the boom must depend on the increased productivity of the land, including the gold and silver. Dean Inge of England observed this and said in 1938, "The house is full." The big house was fuller than the small house was in 1500, and we are now becoming aware of the menace of population growth which concerned nobody as long as the surplus could go to the frontier or be nourished by its ever-increasing bounty. The problem that confronts us in this period of transition from a frontier society to a frontierless world is one that does not trouble the devotees of a popular American game, and that is, what to do with a full house. The validity of the Boom Hypothesis is so abundantly proved by the facts of history and the figures of the statisticians that it seems hardly worthwhile to argue about it.

But there are other less obvious effects of finding a New World. A strange, heady ingredient had suddenly dropped into the mixture we call Western Civilization, an ingredient of such size and potency as to alter the form, texture, the institutions, and the very character of Western society. It gave people a place to go and room to turn around in when they got there. It gave them gold and silver with which to build capitalists; it gave them food to fill every empty belly, to reduce the famines from thirteen to two or three per century; and it gave freedom to those bold enough to take it or even to go to it. It made the medieval world modern, democratic, and capitalistic, and it made the individual the darling of the gods—every man if not a king, at least, a capitalist in his own mind. I realize that this is a broad statement that one should not make if he could not bolster it with evidence and illustrate it with the prevailing trends.

Let us look at some of the trends in Europe from 1500 down to the present, not so much at what was but at what was coming to be. Western civilization tended rapidly to become materialistic because the new ingredient that had been thrown into the mixture was composed of such an abundance of material to be had on such easy terms. The Great Frontier was nearly all material. It tended toward the secular and away from the religious or perhaps the spiritual, because the world suddenly had so much to offer that it had never offered people before. It was such a good place in which to spend a lifetime that men turned to it and away from other-worldliness which had occupied them all during the Middle Ages. It became a world where a man could find his own rewards without regard for divinity or the devil. It became capitalistic. Man was surrounded with the stuff that capital is made of, so much of it that the game of acquiring it became worthwhile. The windfalls were so enormous and the prizes so numerous as to justify any risk. As Bernard DeVoto expressed it, men stumbled over fortunes looking for cows. The prospect of profit was such as to justify the paying of interest; interest paying became honorable as well as profitable without depriving anyone of anything. The Protestants were young and adaptable and they blessed interest long before the tradition-bound ancient Church accepted it, but it finally did. The whole drift of Western civilization from 1500 down to about 1870 was toward individualism. There was never a more favorable climate for the individual than on the frontier. There the man had no choice. He had no protection and no restraint except what he provided for himself. He had to make all decisions for himself and risk the consequences. Democracy which enthrones the individual in politics and makes him of supreme importance to the politicians grew and spread as long as the frontier lasted. The man who is compelled to make his own decisions as to welfare and safety could see no reason why he could not make decisions as to the kind of government he would have, and he wanted one that would guarantee him in the future the freedom he had enjoyed in the past.

And here I want to quote from Herman Melville and a remarkable allegory that he wrote in 1849 called *Mardi*.

187

Melville is speaking of the fact that the old powers had filled up with population and had overflowed their borders. He said:

> And though not yet, have you [the Americans] in any large degree done likewise, it is because you overflow your redundances within your own mighty borders, having a wild western waste, which many shepherds with their flocks could not overrun in a day. Yet overrun at last it will be, and then the recoil must come . . . thus far, your chronicles had narrated a very different story, had your population been pressed and packed, like that of your old sire-land . . . pent up, like them, your thirteen original tribes had proved more turbulent, than so many mutinous legions. Free horses need wide prairies; and fortunate for you . . . that you have room enough, wherein to be free. . . . Civilization has not ever been the brother of equality. Freedom was born among the wide eyries in the mountains . . . you are a great and glorious people. . . . But not wholly because you, in your wisdom decreed it; your origin and geography necessitated it. Nor . . . are all your blessings, to be ascribed to the noble sires, who . . . fought on your behalf. . . . Your nation enjoyed no little independence before your Declaration declared it. Your ancient pilgrims fathered your liberty; and your wild woods harbored the nursling.

The intellectuals of the Western world, as another tendency, turned from authority and dogma to doubt, empiricism, and science. They turned to doubt because the New World presented them with so many truths that they had been taught to deny. They turned to empiricism because the same New World exhibited so many practical things to do; things never done before. They had to be governed by what would work, and in order to find out what would work, they had to tinker and try. You might be interested in being reminded that the only philosophy that America has ever contributed to the world is the philosophy of pragmatism. Pragmatism is defined as the philosophy of what will work. They became scientific because they were presented with a round world instead of a flat one and a lot of other things that surprised them. There were new lands to map, new animals and plants to name, so many that they had to collect, classify, and compare. They were driven to science. It was the wealth of new life forms that led Linnaeus to devise the binomial system of naming living things which is still in use. It was a voyage into the Great Frontier that gave Darwin and Wallace the data on which they jointly built the theory of evolution to change thought and shake orthodoxy. In 1837, the year after Darwin returned on the *Beagle,* he wrote, "In July opened first notebook on Transmutation of Species. Had been greatly struck from about the month of previous March on character of South American fossils, and species on Galapagos. . . . These facts . . . origin of all my views"—facts that he got on the frontier where man had not disturbed the slow change in these animal forms.

The situation is not different in the realm of law, and it was the practical problems arising on the Great Frontier that lead directly to the founding of international law. An obscure professor and theologian in the University of Salamanca achieved immortality of sorts only because the Spanish sovereign asked him to make a study and tell the government how a Christian nation should deal with such primitive pagans as had been found forty years earlier on the American frontier. In answering this practical question, Francisco Vitoria developed the principles of international law and a hundred years later Hugo Grotius formulated these principles and popularized them because he had been retained in a case where the Dutch and Spaniards had clashed on the Far Eastern frontier. Whether we credit Vitoria or Grotius as the father of international law, there is no doubt as to the mother.

As the Great Frontier drove men to be scientific, it lured them toward romance as reflected in literature. Its distance, its mysteries, and its dangers appealed to adventurers and excited the imagination of imaginative men. It was a place about which any romancer could tell lies and have them believed or tell the truth that was more incredulous than the lies. It furnished the stage for Swift's *Gulliver's Travels,* the island for Robinson Crusoe and Friday, another for Robert

189

Louis Stevenson's classic. The long journey across the new seas was the inspiration for Coleridge's "Rime of the Ancient Mariner." It was the theme of Shakespeare's *Tempest*.

I want to turn to something closer to you. It may strain our credulity to be told that the public free school system of the United States had a direct connection with the frontier bounty. But let me remind you that our government in disposing of the public domain set aside land for public education. Not less—and I went to considerable pains to see how much—not less than 211,660 sections were donated to public education and that is enough to make a band eight miles wide around the earth with a strip extending from the Arctic Circle to Patagonia left over—a gift. Every agricultural and mechanical college in America was founded on a land grant. My own university, The University of Texas, received a land subsidy of 2,300,000 acres, or 3,640 sections. From the proceeds of this land the University built its first building and operated the University six years before any legislative appropriation was made for it. Not a brick or a board in a $163 million plant has been paid for by tax money. Income from this land not only built the plant, but as of February 1, 1961, it piled up $376,700,000 in cash and that cash is accumulating at the rate of $17 million per year, often more, and that accumulation, as best as they can judge, will go on for another hundred years from the oil found on this land. It may not yet be counted as a great university but there is nothing comparable to it, possibly excluding California, in the southern half or two thirds of this nation. It is what it is and it is what it will become because of the frontier bounty which it still holds intact.

The frontier not only subsidized public education, colleges, and universities; it subsidized nearly everything else. To railroads in this country it gave an area equal to the size of France. To any farmer it gave 160 acres. To the miners it gave claims. It made western cattle kings by giving free water and free grass. Noting some of these things, William Graham Sumner said, "The very greatest but least noticed significance of the discovery of America was the winning of a new continent for the laboring class." (Really, three and a half new continents.) Emma Lazarus must have seen this when she wrote her famous lines that adorn the Statue of Liberty "Give me your tired, your poor, your huddled masses yearning to be free. Send these, the homeless, tempest-tossed to me; I lift my lamp beside the golden door!"

When Mr. Roosevelt initiated the New Deal in 1933, he put on a pigmy performance in comparison to the new deal that Columbus initiated 441 years earlier. Thus far I have dealt mainly with the manner in which the Great Frontier affected history in the New World. I want to point out one or two examples of how it affected it in Europe and I select two; I admit that they are bizarre and may seem far-fetched. Both of them pertain to a small nation which missed out in the cutting up of the Great Frontier. I refer to Scotland.

About 1690, after the New World had been claimed by the big powers, little Scotland decided to get in on the frontier act. The leader was a William Patterson who conceived that the Panama region was destined to become, as he described it, the crossroads of the world, and he organized a joint stock company, commonly called the Darien Company, and sent it to Darien, which was Spanish territory. Of the five ships sent, only one returned. Had the Spaniards not acted against the Scots, the East India Company and the King in London would have wrecked this enterprise. The Spaniards attacked the Scots, of course, and as they fled north, King William instructed the colonies in the West Indies and on our Atlantic seaboard to give them no aid or relief. The result was that they planted their dead and four of their ships in the Atlantic. The Scots had lost all they invested, about all they had, as well as their kinsmen. They were so infuriated that they became violent, executed an English ship captain, and when they discussed the matter in their parliament, men became incoherent and cried. It was a dangerous situation, and the English decided to do something about it. They must do away with the separate Scottish parliament, merge it with that in London, and the English hired Daniel Defoe, the hack writer, as a public relations man and proceeded by bribery. If Scotland would dissolve the Darien Company, give up all threat to the Great Frontier, and merge their parliament with London, the king would refund to them all the money the nation had invested, with interest at 5 percent for the seven or eight years that their money had been out. The Scottish abnegation occurred in 1707 and is taught to you in history as the Act of Union. Though I have not checked this, it is a safe guess that King William got his slush fund, euphemistically called the equivalent, from the Great Frontier.

A more bizarre incident relates to one of the ships of the Darien Company called the *Rising Sun*. The vessel made it into Charleston, South Carolina, and put in for water and supplies. There was an epidemic of yellow fever in Charleston which kept all on board except one small party. A congregation in Charleston heard that there was a preacher on board named Archibald Stobo. He was invited to come and preach at the white meeting house on the night of September 3, 1700. He accepted, taking his wife with him. It was the season of tropical storms and while the Stobos were absent, the hurricane struck and destroyed the ship and everybody on board. The Rev. Stobo had been saved by Providence, he was naturally called, and he remained in South Carolina. The Stobos had a daughter who married a James Bullock and their son was named Archibald and his son was named James and his son was named James Stephen Bullock and he married an Elliott; as a matter of fact, he married two of them. Now, if you have noticed these names—Archibald, James, and Elliott—you may suspect that we are headed toward a rather prominent American family, and you would be right. James Stephen Bullock had a daughter, Martha, and Martha married Theodore Roosevelt, and they named their son Theodore and this Theodore went out single-handed and took the crossroads of the world that the Scots had failed to take three centuries earlier. Had this Presbyterian minister been the ancestor of another Roosevelt and another president, a great many people would regret that the Stobos did not stay on board the ship.

In citing examples of how the Great Frontier influenced history I am conscious that I have cited facts with which many of you are familiar. Attacking a subject of such magnitude as the Great Frontier, the investigator could not get very far with what is commonly called original or manuscript sources. I think what people *thought* is a source in history. He would be compelled to say what Clark Wissler, the cultural anthropologist, said in his book on *Man and Culture.* He said while it is true that many of the facts cited will be familiar, he was about to look at them in new ways. It was in looking at fairly familiar facts, those in the books, that I hit upon the hypothesis of the new ingredient that altered and transformed Western Civilization. The first thing to do in this situation is to learn whether someone else saw it first. As yet, I have found no one who had advanced the whole hypothesis or attempted to follow it out as I have. Many thinkers have seen part of it, as did Professor Turner, Herman Melville, and William Graham Sumner. Turner saw the American Frontier, a fragment of the Great Frontier and a very important one, but he did not concern himself with the whole. I have found in my own reading that the best thinking on the subject was done by the men who had made the most valuable contributions, men who founded an entire school of thought such as Adam Smith or Sumner and Turner.

Let me cite one or two examples of what people have said about what I call the Great Frontier—they have often called it the New World or they have called it America. The Spanish historian, Francisco Gomara, who wrote in the sixteenth century, said except for the coming of Christ, the most important event since the world began was the discovery of the New World. And Adam Smith had a better understanding, better perhaps than anybody unless it was William Graham Sumner. Smith said that the discovery of America and that of a passage to the East Indies by the Cape of Good Hope are the two greatest and most important events recorded in the history of mankind, and then he goes on to elaborate that in a way that will not do here. R. B. Cunningham-Graham, in describing the effects of relating it to literature, said there has been but one real conquest worthy of the name—that of the New World. The human race in all its annals, holds no record like it. Uncharted seas, unnavigated gulfs, new constellations, the unfathomable black pits of Magellan clouds, the cross hung in the sky, the very need of veering from the poles, islands innumerable, and an unknown world rising out of the sea, all-unsuspected races living in flora never seen by Europeans, made it an achievement unique in the history of mankind.

In his classic study of literature, *The Road to Xanadu*, John Livingston Lowes described the known world prior to Columbus:

> Nothing, I think, is harder to translate into terms of our own blase experience than the present fact that the little pre-Columbian world was islanded in the unknown, and unknown from which came drifting signs and rumors of some knowable beyond. No documents in the world are more eloquent than the laconic legends of the maps.

And what he was referring to there is the dim way these maps appeared, just a suggestion of what the maps are today and their gradual emergence.

When I came upon the last sentence—"No documents in the world are more eloquent than the laconic legends of the maps."—it fired my imagination and I visualized the thrill that must have come to the map-makers as they bent over their drawing boards to chart and shape new continents, islands, gulfs, bays, and rivers as revealed by the returning explorers. And their excitement is shown in the margin by the strange figures with which they peopled the emerging lands.

I have something to say about the reaction of the scholarly world to the thesis that I have advanced—that the Great Frontier has been one of the most powerful forces operating to make Western Civilization what it is today. The reaction has been mixed; not enough time has elapsed to determine whether the idea that I advanced will become a permanent part of intellectual theory, but it is my opinion that it will take twenty-five years for this thesis to be accepted or rejected. Thus far, the concept has moved slowly but at a rather high level. Two years ago an international conference of historians met at The University of Texas to discuss the implications and ramifications of the concept. Scholars were present from England, Spain, Australia, Canada, and several of the Latin American countries. Individuals have been interested and set off on a study of some phase of the subject perhaps I only suggested. One man is writing a book on the impact of the Great Frontier on modern literature, particularly on romantic literature, and this is a tremendous subject. If this work is completed, it could well have to be taken into account by all teachers of literature. A musician at the University of Maryland applied the thesis to the history of music, and he discovered that after 1500 the composition of sacred music declined to almost zero and that the composition of secular music increased from almost zero to its present height. Professor Perry Croft in a volume on historiography gave a chapter to the idea of the Great Frontier.

Now the idea makes slow progress for three reasons, probably more. One, it breaks with tradition and introduces an interpretation different in many respects from earlier ones. It took a long time for Turner's revolutionary idea to take hold. Professors do not take readily to ideas that require them to revise their notes. Second, there are implications involved in the concept that people do not like. I can illustrate this with the Boom Hypothesis I mentioned above. And the reasoning would go something like this: If the opening of the Great Frontier precipitated a four-hundred-year boom, then our modern institutions such as democracy and capitalism and individualism grew up during a boom and are designed to serve a booming society. We look on these institutions as permanent and we hope they are, but the boom is abnormal. Any boom is abnormal even though one may be very long. Therefore, the modern age is abnormal, has turned out of the course that it was following and out of the course somewhat into which it will return, not exactly—you never return completely—and our institutions grew up to meet an abnormal need. They will last as long as the boom lasts and then may give way to a new set of institutions adapted to the new conditions. The boom produced by the Great Frontier will end when the frontier closes. If the frontier produced the boom, then the boom logically would end when the frontier closes. The Frontier in the Western world closed between 1880 and 1910. The institutions that served it now fail or have to be radically modified. People do not like those questions. They do not like to face them and they do not like the way you answer unless you answer in a way that they like. The idea that there is no longer a frontier is unpleasant to many people. It is slightly unpleasant to me. We are homesick for it and we want it back with all its windfalls, and its opportunities and its freedom; and because we have lost it, we are always hunting for new frontiers. We see them in space, in education, in missionary work—everywhere that somebody wants to go. Senator John Kennedy evoked this frontier emotion in his campaign for the presidency and probably got many votes by promising new frontiers. Most of these new frontiers are fallacious, I suspect, including Mr. Kennedy's. They are not frontiers at all. But even if they are, the conditions of taking them are so different from those existing in our own history as to create a revolution, even if they be frontiers. They will not be taken by man in the Studebaker wagon or on a horse. What we have to learn is to live without the kind of frontier we had for four centuries.

In conclusion, I want to call your attention to the difficulty in introducing a new idea. In making a study of the dispersion of the Great Frontier by the sovereigns of Europe (and what I mean was the explorers claimed these continents, claimed them in the name of the sovereigns and then they had to distribute the finds), I saw that they did it on a free, or nearly free, basis. The sovereigns virtually gave to the people over a period of three or more centuries, forty million quarter-sections of land. This was a relief program of gigantic proportions; in watching this distribution, I derived the theory of the vertical pulsation of wealth in the modern state. The economists have dealt with wealth as if it had but one motion, that is circulation from John Doe to Richard Roe. That, I call the horizontal motion of wealth. But throughout modern times, at any rate, wealth had a vertical motion, flowing from sovereign to the people, primarily. This went on until there was no more frontier and until there was nothing to distribute, until the cupboard was bare. Then, and not until then, did the sovereign have to take from you in order to have something to give to me. When Mr. Roosevelt introduced the New Deal he merely found a new technique for continuing a give-away program that began in 1500. All of your ancestors here in Indiana—not all of them but a great many of them—received free 160 acre homesteads. You did not know you were on relief; you thought you were being heroes. But it was relief just the same, as if you had received a job in 1933, and the operation was so big, though, that people have overlooked it. But I want to come back to this circulation of wealth. I thought that the economists would be interested in the fact that they had overlooked the vertical motion of wealth, that is between the sovereign and the people, having made their interpretation in terms of one motion, the horizontal. Though the book has now been available for some time, no economist that I know of has read it.

Nearly every thinker agrees finally that we are now at

the end of an era in history and at the beginning of another era, the nature of which we can only guess at. If we *are* at the end of an age, the one we are leaving can no longer be called modern. We will have to find another name. For me, an appropriate name for the period from 1500 to the present would be The Age of the Great Frontier.

FOOTNOTES

AN EXPLANATION

[1] "An Honest Preface" in which Dr. Webb, tongue-in-cheek, pays oblique respects to orthodoxy in book introductions is not included in this volume because it is available elsewhere. It first appeared as an essay in the *Southwest Review*, Vol. XXXVI, No. 4, pp. 312–314, Autumn, 1951. See also *An Honest Preface and Other Essays*, Boston, Houghton Mifflin Company, 1959, with its inimitable introduction by Joe B. Frantz. Incidentally, though formalism requires that reference be made to "Webb" or "W. P. Webb" or "Walter Prescott Webb," it is with difficulty that the handle to his name is abandoned. To most who knew him, he was Dr. Webb, and to refer to him otherwise seems, in a sense, to be less majesty.

[2] *Harper's Magazine*, Vol. CCXIII, No. 1334 (July, 1961). Condensed and reprinted, *Reader's Digest*, Vol. 79, No. 472 (August, 1961).

[3] *Texas Libraries* (Austin), Vol. 25, No. 3, pp. 82–87 (Fall, 1963).

[4] *Webb, A Catalogue of Books from the Library of Walter Prescott Webb, 1888–1963*, Catalogue No. 50. The Brick Row Book Shop, Austin, 1964, pp. 3–12.

[5] The University of Texas Press, Austin, 1968.

[6] "Hypothesis in History," undated mimeographed typescript.

[7] "The Art of Historical Writing," mimeographed typescript dated 1964 [*sic*], p. 15.

CHAPTER II

[1] Apparently Turner had a little trouble in making his Wisconsin subject palatable to the Johns Hopkins professors. Fulmer Mood, after stating that

Herbert Baxter Adams directed Turner's dissertation, says: "Adams did not think that the West had institutions worthy of study, but he permitted the young man from Wisconsin to follow his own bent. Institutional history . . . was the style of Johns Hopkins, and Turner wrote . . . on the trading post as an institution. He was able to demonstrate in learned fashion, and perhaps with . . . tongue in . . . cheek, that the trading post could be followed back into Phoenician and Roman time." Fulmer Mood, "Turner's Formative Period," *The Early Writings of Frederick Jackson Turner* (Madison, Wisconsin: Wisconsin University Press, 1938), 20.

2 Turner quotes from Loria's *Analisis della proprieta capitalisti* (2 vols., Turin, 1889), II, 15, as follows: "America has the key to the historical enigma which Europe has sought for centuries in vain, and the land which has no history reveals luminously the course of universal history." See Turner's footnote 23, page 207, in the 1893 essay "The Significance of the Frontier in American History," in American Historical Association, *Annual Report*, 1893 (Washington, D.C., 1894), 199–227.

3 *The Economic Foundations of Society*, Keasbey (New York, 1899), 123. Loria published the first edition of this work in 1885. The above sentence is taken from the revised edition in 1899, the only one available to me.

CHAPTER III

1 Erwin Hinckley Barbour, *Wells and Windmills in Nebraska*, Water Supply and Irrigation Papers, No. 29, U.S. Geological Survey, Washington, 1899.

CHAPTER IV

1 *The Great Frontier*, Houghton Mifflin Company, 1952.

CHAPTER VIII

1 Herbert Baxter Adams, "New Methods of Study in History," *Johns Hopkins University Studies in Historical and Political Science* (Baltimore), II (1884), 107.

2 Edward G. Bourne, "Leopold von Ranke," American Historical Association, *Annual Report*, 1896 (2 vols., Washington, 1897), I, 71.

3 Historians of contemporary times are appalled by the volume of documents. In a lecture in Austin, Texas, April 8, 1953, Arnold Toynbee stated that the British documents pertaining to World War II would fill a shelf eighteen miles long. Ancient historians are handicapped by a paucity of documents, contemporary historians by a plethora. Ranke hit on a period when they were abundant but still manageable.

4 For a treatment of the evolution of the German schools of "scientific" history from Ranke on, see James Westfall Thompson, *A History of Historical Writing* (2 vols., New York, 1942), II, Chaps. XLII and XLIII. Thompson denies that Ranke himself was objective.

5 Michael Kraus, *The Writing of American History* (Norman, Okla., 1953), 5.

6 Bourne, "Leopold von Ranke," American Historical Association, *Annual Report*, 1896, I, 67–80.

7 Thompson, *History of Historical Writing*, II, 238.

8 Margaret M. Spector, "A. P. Newton," in Herman Ausubel, J. Bartlet Brebner, and Erling M. Hung (eds.), *Some Modern Historians of Britain: Essays in Honor of R. L. Schuyler* (New York, 1951), 293.

9 Quoted in Bourne, "Leopold von Ranke," American Historical Association, *Annual Report*, 1896, I, 72.

[10] *Ibid.*, 73.

[11] Quoted in Thompson, *History of Historical Writing*, II, 188.

[12] Fustel de Coulanges is reported to have said: "It requires years of analysis for a day of synthesis."

[13] Thompson, *History of Historical Writing*, II, 230.

[14] This account is based on Arnold J. Toynbee, *A Study of History* (10 vols., London, 1934–1954), X, 12 ff. Any historian who is hesitating to take a chance on an original idea should read Toynbee's last volume, which bears the title, "The Inspiration of Historians."

[15] Kraus, *Writing of American History*, 165.

[16] Henry Adams, *The Education of Henry Adams: An Autobiography* (Boston, 1918), 75.

[17] *Ibid.*, 81.

[18] *Ibid.*, 77.

[19] *Ibid.*, 76.

[20] *Ibid.*, 300.

[21] *Ibid.*, 302.

[22] *Ibid.*, 303.

[23] Carson Ryan, *Studies in Early Graduate Education* (New York, 1939), 32.

[24] *Ibid.*, 29.

[25] Herbert Baxter Adams, "New Methods of Study in History," *Journal of Social Science* (New York), XVIII (May, 1884), 251 ff.

[26] Kraus, *Writing of American History*, 286–287.

[27] For an account of the business activities of Schliemann, Leaf, Grote, and Rhodes, see Toynbee, *Study of History*, X, 145 ff.

[28] John W. Caughey, *Hubert Howe Bancroft: Historian of the West* (Berkeley, 1946), vii, says: "In the historiography of the West, no name is written larger than Hubert Howe Bancroft's." For Bancroft's account of his method see *The Works of Hubert Howe Bancroft* (39 vols., San Francisco, 1882–1890), XXXIX. This volume was also published separately as *Literary Industries: A Memoir* (New York, 1891).

[29] Here I wish to say a word on behalf of young men, especially in the large universities, who are driven to write when they have nothing to say and fired if they do not say it with documentation. The system is vicious and is providing an oversupply of beer-keg makers. I have devised a substitute system for universities to consider. That would be for the university to pay a flat sum to the young teacher for his services as a teacher and put him on a piece-basis for his so-called production. This would require a scale, a bonus system which would automatically register the worth of the harried young man and relieve his superior from making decisions.

Let us say that the base pay for teaching is $4,500. In addition, here is what the young man gets for production: Full length book, $500; monograph, $100; book review, $15; paper before learned society, $25. For evidence of recognition by his peers, apply this scale: Favorable review of his book, $10.00; unfavorable review, 50 cents; quotation by another author, $5.00 each; reference in footnote, $2.00 each; listing in bibliography, $1.00. All rates would be doubled for foreign publications. This would be a reversal of a system already started of taking from the scholar all he earns outside his salary, a system which I trust will not spread to other institutions.

[30] Francis M. Cornford, *Microcosmographia Academica, Being a Guide for the Young Academic Politician* (3rd ed., Cambridge, England, 1933), 47.

INDEX

204